From
THE
Heart

Eight Rules to Live By

From
THE
Heart

Eight Rules to Live By

ROBIN ROBERTS

HYPERION

NEW YORK

The Library of Congress has cataloged the hardcover edition of
this book as follows:

Roberts, Robin
      From the heart : Seven rules to live by / Robin Roberts.—1st
   ed.
         p. cm.
      ISBN 1-4013-0333-1
      ISBN 13: 978-14013-0333-4
         1. Success—Psychological aspects. 2. Roberts, Robin, 1960-
      I. Title.
   BF637.S8R5785 2007
   158—dc22   2006049705

Paperback ISBN: 978-1-4013-0958-9

Hyperion books are available for special promotions, premiums,
or corporate training. For details contact Michael Rentas, Pro-
prietary Markets, Hyperion, 77 West 66th Street, 12th floor,
New York, New York 10023, or call 212-456-0133.

Design by James Sinclair

FIRST PAPERBACK EDITION

10 9 8 7 6 5 4 3 2 1

This book is dedicated to
Lawrence and Lucimarian Roberts
for giving their baby girl wings—and being
the wind beneath those wings,
making it possible for me to soar to heights
I never could have imagined for myself.
(Even fighting cancer!)
I love you with all my heart.

Contents

Contents

Introduction:
From the Heart

I had no idea that one day I would write a book. I also had no idea that one day I would be the coanchor of *Good Morning America*. Isn't it wonderful how life can surprise you?

I remember my first morning as coanchor. The announcer said: "This is *Good Morning America* with Charles Gibson, Diane Sawyer, and Robin Roberts." All of a sudden I was on camera sitting next to Charlie and Diane. I wanted to shout to the TV audience, "I don't know how I got here either!"

Some part of me was thinking: Why would people listen to what I had to say? What had I experienced and learned in my life that I could impart to viewers? Then Hurricane Katrina hit right in my hometown, and I was thrust into the heart of it. *GMA* became a way for me to reach out and make a difference. I found my voice, and the viewers responded.

I have to admit, though, when my editor at Hyperion, Gretchen Young, told me they wanted to frame this book as my "rules to live by," I laughed.

"Right," I said, "Roberts's Rules of Order." As if *I* could give people rules for life. That wasn't me. I always felt like a person who had broken all the rules—and the mold they came in too. I was a woman, I was black, and I didn't care if people said I didn't belong in sports or broadcasting. I pushed my way in. So the idea of writing rules tickled me.

But as I thought about it, I realized that in another sense rules were a big part of my life—before I broke them.

When I was young I was totally focused on being an athlete, and I was the type of athlete who always played by the rules. Maybe the fact that my father was in the Air Force for more than thirty years has something to do with that. You don't retire as a full colonel in the United States Air Force without playing by the rules. My father instilled those values in his four children. (I'm the baby of the family.)

It wasn't just rules for the sake of rules. We learned that rules have a purpose. They teach us invaluable lessons. Lessons that we may not even be aware of at the time, like discipline. It's not always easy to do what is expected of us, especially when others aren't holding up their end of the bargain. But my parents never let us get away with measuring ourselves against other people's performance or blaming someone else's failure for our own. Our house was a no-whine zone. We were taught to take responsibility for our own actions.

When I was a freshman basketball player at Southeastern Louisiana University, my coach, Linda Puckett, devised a challenging drill. She instructed the team to stay in a crouched position as we slid all the way around the court. We were not to stand up until we reached a certain point. I was in the middle of the pack as we did the drill. When we were finished, Coach Puckett got right in my face and said, "Hon, you are going places in life." It turned out that I was the only one who remained in the crouched position for the entire time.

I could have easily been like everyone else on my team and come out of the uncomfortable position before I was supposed to. It took discipline, determination, and stamina to stay put. Traits that come in handy in life, whether you're on the basketball court, on the job, or raising a family.

When I was a child watching *Good Morning America*, I could never have imagined sitting in that anchor chair. A life in broadcasting wasn't even on my radar. My total focus was on becoming a professional athlete. But looking back, I am convinced that I would have been successful at anything I pursued, because of my sports background. For as long as I can remember, I've loved sports. I am always fascinated by how fast I can run, how far I can throw a ball, how high I can jump. That was especially true when I was younger. When I was twelve years old, I was the state bowling champ in Mississippi. I still remember the headline in the local paper: PETITE BOWLER TAKES STATE TITLE. I think it was the one and only time I have ever been called petite.

Growing up on the Mississippi Gulf Coast, I loved all sports, but tennis was my first true passion. Oh, how I would daydream about one day taking center court at Wimbledon! I imagined myself curtsying to the queen and eating strawberries and cream. But even though my heart belonged to tennis, my body was more suited for basketball. When you're 5'10" in the eighth grade, people expect you to play hoops, so that's what I did. I put my heart into the game and loved it. And although I didn't realize my dream of becoming a professional athlete, those experiences on the court never left me. In fact, they became an integral part of me.

The principles I learned through sports prepared me for success. They taught me certain rules that I live by to this day:

1. *Position yourself to take the shot.* I learned how to put myself in position for good things to happen to me. Even when I felt outmatched or afraid, I made sure I was ready to grab the ball when it came my way.

2. *Dream big, but focus small.* When I was young I had big dreams, and my parents, teachers, and coaches encouraged me. But they also helped me to see that I had to have my feet planted in reality. Dreams are vague and far away. Goals are tangible and achievable.

I learned that being true to myself meant figuring out what was right for me, then pursuing it.

3. *If at first you don't succeed, dive back in.* Here's a secret. It isn't always the smartest, most talented, prettiest, or most charismatic person who has the most success. That's true whether you're talking about a great job, a great achievement, or a great marriage. More often, the people who succeed are those who don't let setbacks and rejections stop them cold.

4. *Never play the race, gender, or any other card.* The most valuable lesson my parents taught me was that there is no excuse for not being the best you can be. When you fail, don't look for fault in others; find the areas you need to improve in yourself. And don't be too thin-skinned. Learn to laugh at your frailties. We all have them.

5. *Venture outside your comfort zone.* To stop growing is to stop living. My parents taught me this lesson by taking new chances late in their lives. When you look at your life as a work in progress every day, nothing is impossible.

6. *Focus on the solution, not the problem.* We all have problems, and it's easy to let them drag you down. The key to lifting yourself up is to focus on what action you can take to solve them. You may be taking baby steps, but they move you forward.

7. *Keep faith, family, and friends close to your heart.* My life has been filled with blessings—a deep faith, strong family ties, and a core group of friends who support and challenge me. My faith, family, and friends are the foundation upon which everything else rests. True success cannot be measured by the fleeting façades of fame and money, but only by the underlying security of a life well lived.

After I deliver a speech I am often asked for a copy of it. The problem is I never write my speeches. I just talk. That is my hope for this book. It's just me talking to you. Talking about the things I have learned that have helped me find joy in my life and fulfillment in my work.

Trust me when I tell you that I am not the brightest person in the world. And trust me, my friends would wholeheartedly agree! There is no magical reason why I am where I am. And there is absolutely no reason why you can't be where you want to be. If it can happen for me, it can happen for you, too. And it would be a privilege for me to help you get there.

But wait! There's an important new eighth rule— Make Your Mess Your Message. Please look for an all-new chapter at the back of the book.

From
THE
Heart

Eight Rules to Live By

1. Position Yourself to Take the Shot

I'm a big believer that you have to put yourself in position for good things to happen to you. You can dream, hope, and pray all you want, but if you're not ready when opportunity calls, it will pass you by. Often, the person who catches the break isn't the most capable or talented, but the one who is standing there with his or her arms outstretched at the right moment.

This was a constant lesson for me growing up, because we moved around a lot. My father was in the Air Force, and we traveled all over the world when I was a kid. My siblings and I were each born in different states—Ohio, Arizona, Iowa, and Alabama. One of my dad's favorite assignments was being stationed in Izmir, Turkey, in the late 1960s. He thought it would be good for the family, and he was right. What a beautiful country—rich in history and culture. Instead of living on a military base with other Americans, my parents decided we would live in an apartment in town. They wanted their children to experience a different culture. My best friends were Turkish, and they taught me how to speak their language and play their games. My parents were constantly looking for creative ways to educate us. By immersing us in a different culture, they helped us become more tolerant and compassionate. They opened our eyes to the world.

Whenever it came time to pack up and move again, my parents would play a little game with us. They'd give us the first letter of the place we were moving to and make us guess the answer. So, after two and a half years in Izmir, they sat us down and said, "OK, kids, we're moving back to the States to a place that begins with the letter M." We shouted, "Montana, Maine, Michigan, Missouri!" Nope. We racked our little brains and hesitantly asked, "Mississippi?" Yep. Well, we threw a fit. We wailed that there was *no way* we would go there. It was 1969, and the Magnolia State wasn't exactly appealing to the Roberts children.

But when we moved to Biloxi, Mississippi, we were pleasantly surprised. Despite our initial objections—which included a lot of temper tantrums—the Mississippi Gulf Coast was a wonderful place to grow up. We instantly fell in love with this picturesque region and its lovely, caring people—not to mention the unbelievable food. And it was in Biloxi that my devotion to sports blossomed.

When my father retired in 1975, my parents decided to stay. Of all the places in the world they had lived, this one felt the most like home. They bought a house in Pass Christian, a small town about twenty miles from Biloxi, along the beautiful Gulf Coast. Locals affectionately refer to it as "the Pass."

I was just starting high school, which was housed in a charming redbrick building. It was the only high school in town, and most of the kids had been friends since the first grade. At first they didn't know what to make of me—this tall girl who came bounding into their lives. It's never easy to break into the tight-knit circle of small-town friendships, but I had two things going for me. First, because I was used to moving to new schools, I wasn't shy. I knew I could make people laugh, and the force of humor can never be underestimated. Second, I played basketball. Through basketball I met two girls who would become my lifelong friends. The first time I walked into the auditorium, Cheryl Antoine and Luella Fairconeture looked me up and down like *"Who's this?"* I was wearing some awful outfit—green plaid, as I recall. Cheryl later said she was immediately appraising my height for the team. She laughed, recalling. "I thought, 'Are those legs ever going to stop?'"

I quickly wore down any resistance that existed and became a fixture in the school. Cheryl, Luella, and I became so tight we called ourselves the "True Blues." Of course, at first I had a little trouble understanding that warm Southern drawl. For the longest time, when I was on the basketball court, I thought the cheerleaders were chanting:

Eat potted meat.
Get up off your feet.

I just thought it was some kind of strange Southern custom. Finally, I asked Cheryl, "What is potted meat? Is it a special meat you all have down here?" She looked at me like I'd lost my mind. When I explained about the cheer, she laughed so hard she had to sit down. It turned out they were chanting:

Leap, Robin, leap.
Get up off your feet.

Back when I'd started playing basketball in the eighth grade, at first I didn't have to work all that hard, because I towered over everybody else. But by the time I reached high school, I suddenly wasn't the tallest player on the court. That's when I learned the importance of position.

Our coaches always emphasized that in order to score, we had to get into the proper position to make it happen. If we wanted to get a rebound, we needed to get into the proper rebounding position. If we wanted to hit a topspin forehand, we needed to get into the proper position for that. It wasn't enough to hope for a rebound or a score. We had to work our tails off getting situated to make it happen.

If we were playing a team that clearly was better, our coach told us, "At least put yourself in position to win. Don't give up before the game even starts. Do whatever you have to do to keep the score close. Then if you get some lucky breaks late in the game, you can win. If you don't even try, and fall way behind, those lucky breaks won't do you any good."

Our coaches also stressed that when we took the court against an opponent who was superior, we had to have heart. An opponent could be stronger and have better skills, and we couldn't help that. But there was no excuse for not wanting victory as much as they did. That is a matter of heart. Why else are we so enamored with the story of David versus Goliath?

I played a lot of basketball games when I was in high school and college, but there's one game in particular that I'll never forget. It was my junior year of college, and we were playing a team that always dominated. They were the big school, and the girls seemed bigger too. The players had a swagger about them that went beyond confidence. They looked at us like we were bugs. They had never lost to us. And just that one time I wanted so badly to beat them. I wanted to do some damage to that swagger.

I had a good game, but as we got toward the end, we were down by six points. We needed the ball back. I purposely fouled a player who was one of the cockiest girls on the team. She took her place on the line to shoot the free throws, and as I watched her I saw that her knees were shaking. A couple of her teammates came up to her and she started screeching, "Get away, get away!" She was a wreck.

I remember thinking, "Hey, you're not so tough." I must have been grinning from ear to ear.

And sure enough, she missed the free throws, and we ended up winning the game. It was sweet.

I never forgot that game, because I realized that people are not always as together as they may seem. They can have a pretty convincing façade, but as soon as they're in danger of losing, the façade cracks like an egg. Once they're exposed, it's not so pretty.

I've learned that it's the people who have been tested and have persevered who you want to watch. I remember the great prizefighter Floyd Patterson once saying, "I've been knocked down more than any heavyweight champion in history." But, he added, "I've gotten up more than any heavyweight champion in history. Don't forget that."

I've applied the same principle to every challenge I've faced. It is the number-one rule I live by. I don't shy away from difficulties. If I get knocked down, I get back up. I at least give myself an opportunity. I don't quit the game when I fall behind. I have always believed that if I hang in there and keep the "score" close, I'll be in a position to benefit from the lucky breaks. Proximity is power.

The Mississippi Gulf Coast isn't exactly the center of the universe, but that didn't mean there weren't possibilities. It tickles me that some people think you have to be from a big city to "make it." There are opportunities everywhere. Instead of worrying about whether you'll ever get that big break, spend time preparing yourself so you'll be ready to benefit from each opportunity that comes along.

It meant a lot to me when my classmates named me Miss Pass Christian High in my senior year. It made me realize that nine out of ten times, people will accept you and encourage you if you let them. You can always "belong" wherever you are.

Positioning yourself to win isn't always so easy. In a flash doubts can creep in, and before you know it you can start wavering and lose your focus. When that happens, the key is finding a way to keep your eye on the ball.

Last year I had the opportunity to visit Julie Foudy's girls' soccer camp in New Jersey. Julie was a member of the 1999 World Cup team that captivated the nation—especially little girls. It was a leadership camp, with twelve- to sixteen-year-olds from all over the country. The theme was "Live, Lead, and Pass It On." Julie invited me to give the campers a pep talk and share a few of my experiences. I welcomed the chance to talk to these young girls and hopefully give them something solid and inspirational to take away with them. The girls were gathered around, asking me questions, and one of them asked, "Have you always been sure of yourself? Was there ever a time that you doubted yourself?" I could see by the intense expression on her face that she really wanted to know—I guessed because she herself had experienced doubts.

"Absolutely," I assured her. "Everyone has doubts sometimes. And I mean everyone."

She looked relieved. I get this all the time from young people. They assume that doubts are a sign of weakness, and all the truly great people in the world don't have them. The truth is, we're all pretty fragile to begin with. There are only a very few people who are cocky sons of guns straight out of the womb. And they're not always the most successful. I think I worry more about someone who *never* has doubts.

Most of us struggle with thinking we're not good enough. I always said that if I was the smartest or most talented person on the team, we were in big trouble! What makes the difference between success and failure is not whether you have doubts, but what you do when the doubts creep in. And they will. How do you get past them? What works for me is taking action. Doing something tangible to get myself into position. I can't control everything that happens, but I can be ready.

I didn't just learn this key principle through sports. My parents were a huge inspiration. My dad was showing the way before I was even born. You see, when my dad was a young boy, in the 1930s, he dreamed of flying airplanes one day. He'd take a broomstick handle and put it between his legs and imagine he was flying. People told him he was crazy. A black man would never be allowed to fly a plane.

Remember, back then African Americans didn't have those kinds of opportunities. But my dad refused to listen to the naysayers. Instead, he learned everything he could about aviation. He sought out the chance to do what he loved, and he refused to accept defeat. He joined the military, and became one of the famous Tuskegee Airmen—the first black American air corps. The Tuskegee Airmen flew 1,578 missions during World War II. They never lost a single plane they escorted into battle.

My dad positioned himself for success. He had the career he dreamed of. He traveled the world on exciting assignments. He proudly served in three wars for his country. He gave his family the opportunities he'd never had growing up. He made sure his children were in a position to succeed.

My mother is also an inspiration. It still amazes me when I think about the quiet, steady way she pursued her goals. Her parents never went beyond the sixth grade. My mom was the first in her family to go to college. She attended Howard University on a $100 scholarship. But like most women of her era, she didn't really set goals for herself beyond having a family. As she once said, laughing, when someone asked her what she majored in at Howard, "I majored in extracurricular activities and I minored in finding a husband."

Mom never pursued a career outside the home while we were growing up, yet today, at age eighty-four, she is a polished woman whose credentials are awe-inspiring. She was the first woman to serve as president of the Mississippi Coast Coliseum Commission, the first woman to chair the Mississippi State Board of Education, and the first woman to serve as a member of the board of directors of the Mississippi Power Company. She also served as chairperson of the New Orleans branch of the Federal Reserve Bank of Atlanta. And she did all of this *after* her children were grown!

Come on, think about it. Here she was, approaching sixty; she'd never really had a career outside the home—I asked my mom recently how'd she do it? Inquiring minds wanted to know.

She answered simply, "Well, when your father retired from the Air Force and we moved to the Pass, the first thing I wanted to do was get involved in politics. And my involvement in politics led to other things. I became acquainted with the governor . . ."

"Wait a minute," I interrupted. "How did you become acquainted with the governor? Here you were, a housewife in Mississippi who had never had a career."

"Well," she replied, "I became acquainted with the governor because I was willing to take an active role in the community. I became the Harrison County Democratic Executive Chairperson. And with that, I met the governor. When he had an opportunity to appoint me, first he appointed me to the children's rehab center in Jackson. And I enjoyed that very much. That was my first appointment. And then all of the mayors along the Gulf Coast selected me as their representative to be a commissioner for the Coliseum. So that was another stepping stone. From the Coliseum, I was appointed to the Federal Reserve. The governor then had an opportunity to appoint lay board members, so I became part of the lay board. And I've always been interested in children and their education, so that was a stepping stone to helping me move into other areas."

She makes it sound obvious and easy. My mother is pretty humble about her remarkable capabilities. But one thing is plain: She positioned herself to achieve. The opportunities didn't just come to her out of the blue. In fact, when I look at what Mom made of her life, given all the barriers she had to overcome, I am truly proud. I'm also grateful because I feel she put her dreams on hold so Dad and her children could pursue theirs.

Mom rose from poverty to prosperity. She grew up in Akron, Ohio, where her family was devastated by the Depression of the 1930s. It didn't help that her father, my Grandfather Tolliver, was an alcoholic. My dear grandmother, Grandma Sally, worked as a maid, a cook, a babysitter—whatever she could find. The most she ever earned was a dollar a day. Mom remembers a particular summer evening in Akron when she was six years old. Grandma Sally was cooking dinner on a potbelly stove in the basement. All the utilities in the house had been cut off because they could no longer afford to pay for them. As Grandma Sally cooked, the family sat around a makeshift dining-room table in the basement, lit by the glow of a kerosene lamp.

Lucimarian was a precocious child. (I guess having me later was her payback.) She wanted to make her parents feel better, so she announced, "I have a song in my heart, and I'm going to sing it!"

My unemployed grandfather was not amused. He told her, "Not at this table you're not!" So what did Mom do? She gobbled down her dinner and raced outside. When she reached the basement window, she sank to her knees and serenaded her family through the screen window. It was that unconquerable spirit that carried my mom to unimaginable heights.

Because of my mom's example, her brother, William, went to college on the G.I. Bill and became a certified public accountant. Her sister, Depholia, became a nurse. And her father turned to Alcoholics Anonymous. By the time I was born, Grandpa Tolliver was sober. I never remember him drinking. I do remember him reading from the Bible as he ministered to other alcoholics. Perhaps my grandfather would have found Alcoholics Anonymous even had my mother not excelled in life. But I strongly believe that seeing his daughter position herself for success gave him a greater confidence that he could too.

Today, when people ask me for the secret of my success, I say, "Being born to Lawrence and Lucimarian Roberts!"

My parents taught me through their example that

any individual can succeed. Don't get stuck in that awful trap of thinking others with more material advantages or happier childhoods or better educations have more of what it takes to get ahead. The secret to succeeding is to find it from within. We all see plenty of examples of people who seem to have it all, yet they're not happier or more successful at life. And we see other examples of people who rise above unbelievable challenges to make it.

Last year on *Good Morning America*, I had the chance to do a feature about a remarkable forty-six-year-old man named Donald Mingo. His story is the kind that sticks with you. Donald was born deaf and was unable to speak. Then he was stricken with polio as a child and had to learn to walk again. I knew I had to meet this man after I learned that the Honda dealership in Levittown, New York, where he'd worked for twenty years, was throwing him a twentieth-anniversary party.

Donald's job was washing, waxing, and detailing new cars for customer pickup. In twenty years, he had missed only three days of work! His boss praised him for his dedication and said he wished Donald had a brother. Donald's coworkers were clearly fond of him and appreciated his hard work. When he made those cars shine, he made *them* shine.

What I found most remarkable about Donald was his sheer joy and enthusiasm. He was one of the happiest people I'd ever met. He wasn't sitting around feeling gypped by life. He considered himself blessed, and he lived the life of a blessed man.

People like Donald Mingo teach us that the key to success lies within. No matter who you are, chances are that at one time or another you have been successful at something. You set your sights on a goal and you attained it. How did you do it? Apply the same principles to the challenge before you now. Consider it your personal formula for success.

Our actions, inactions, words, or silence can have major consequences, good and bad. How much do you want to succeed? What is it you want to accomplish? Whether it's a different position at work, a new career, or a stronger relationship with your family, put yourself in position to get it. Don't just dream about it. Don't just wish for it. Make it happen. You can.

While we're on the subject of positioning yourself

for success, I have a word of advice for mothers and fathers. I know how much you all want your children to do well in life and to have every opportunity possible. But don't take this to mean that you have to be hypervigilant about every step your child takes, for fear that he or she will miss out. Today, there's so much pressure on young kids. It breaks my heart when I see people getting wound up in knots because their kid didn't get into a top preschool, or when I watch high school students sweating bullets because they really haven't figured out what they want to do with their lives. The job of being a kid is to explore and experiment and learn. It's the time you have to work out who you are. That's hard to do if you're under constant pressure to perform. I know the world is a competitive place, but I believe the child who is allowed to find his or her own way—even when that means failing and trying again—will be a stronger person in adulthood than the child who follows the prescribed path others set.

If you're the mother of daughters, one of the best gifts you can give them is to encourage them to participate in sports. Playing sports is empowering. Surely you remember being a little girl. It's tough. You're just naturally insecure. Playing sports, feeling the competitive drive, winning and losing—these experiences build self-esteem and character. Little boys have been benefiting from their sports training forever. Think about it. Guys are amazing. They can tear each other up one minute, then go out for a beer together the next. Sports gives them that perspective. Women can be timid because they get stuck in the feeling that they have to be liked and have to please everyone to get ahead. I assure you, sports shakes that out of you. On the court or on the field, you don't care if the other team *likes* you. You just want to win. It makes you stronger. So, if you want to do your daughters a huge favor, introduce them to sports. It's the best training ground for adult life.

I never stop appreciating how fortunate we are to live in these times when young girls can actually visualize pursuing careers in sports. I often think of my Grandma Sally, six feet tall and a natural athlete, who came into the world during an era when that door was not open. Sally loved sports, and I'm sure I inherited the sports gene from her. Grandma Sally passed away in 1991, just shy of her ninety-first birthday, but I can still picture her glued to her radio, giving the players a piece of her mind when they didn't perform. She loved listening to renowned sportscaster Red Barber, and although she lived in Ohio, she was a huge Dallas Cowboys fan. Man, was she angry when Tom Landry, the legendary coach of the Cowboys, was callously dumped in favor of Jimmy Johnson. Grandma admired how Landry always wore a suit on the sidelines. She thought he looked quite dapper wearing his trademark hat. Grandma thought it was silly that baseball managers wore uniforms like the players. She would laugh and say, "What are they gonna do? Put themselves in the lineup and play with those young whippersnappers?"

When I went to work at ESPN, Grandma Sally was bursting with pride. She picked up the phone and called her local newspaper to announce, "My granddaughter is a sportscaster at ESPN!" She even got cable TV for the first time in her life. She had no idea where the cable outlet was in her home. When she found it, she had to rearrange the furniture in her living room to accommodate the TV. Grandma Sally was thrilled to see her dreams fulfilled through me. But how much better it is that we now live in a time when a woman can fulfill her dreams for herself.

The pace of change is slow, and women have had to struggle to overcome many barriers. But in the last century we've succeeded in knocking them down, one at a time. I'll bet that future generations will look back and be astonished that we made such a big deal about whether a woman could be president.

The seeds of future possibility are planted every day in the lives of young women, and sports has a lot to do with that. It's a catalyst. I remember so vividly being at the Rose Bowl for the deciding match of the 1999 World Cup, when the American women's team beat China. As I walked into the parking lot early that morning, it was a wild scene. There were tailgate parties, and teenage boys were walking around with MIA and JULIE painted across their chests. The stadium was packed with 90,000 people—and forty million more were watching from home. Those soccer players were like twelve Michael Jordans. Everyone wanted their autographs. It had to make such a tremendous and lasting impression on those young girls watching from home. They were witnessing women being celebrated for their strength and determination—not for their appearance.

Seeing the drive and intelligence of the girls at Julie Foudy's soccer camp, I recalled that Christine Brennan, a reporter for *USA Today*, once observed that someday there *will* be a woman president. And when she's asked what the defining moment of her childhood was, she'll say, "The 1999 Women's World Cup."

2. Dream Big, but Focus Small

I have always asked myself: What is the one thing I can do today to get me closer to my goal? I prefer to set goals for myself rather than to dream. You can write goals down on a piece of paper. Somehow they feel more attainable that way.

As I've said, as a young girl I had a passion for sports. I dreamed of being a pro. But it was just that—a dream. In high school I faced reality. I was not going to be a pro athlete when I grew up. I was the best doggone average athlete you've ever met. Desire and passion will take you only so far in sports. There's a little something called *ability* that you must have. Don't get me wrong, I was pretty good. By the time I was a senior I was All-State, but I was bright enough to know that I'd had too late a start to think of playing basketball professionally. I didn't start playing basketball until the eighth grade. The majority of women you see in the WNBA have been playing ball from the time they learned how to walk! For a while I continued to have dreams of playing pro tennis. I would read every tennis publication cover to cover, again and again, until the pages were practically falling apart in my hands. Mom would say, "You know, there's another issue next month." At one point I hired a coach and played in some special tournaments. Once again the awful truth revealed itself: This was not going to be my career.

I started panicking a little bit. What could I do? I still wanted to pursue a profession involving sports. Preferably a career that had the same characteristics— competition, travel, excitement. Something that would push me and test me constantly. My oldest sister, Sally-Ann, is a reporter and an anchor for a TV station in New Orleans. Sally-Ann is eight years older than I am, and I was always impressed with how certain she was of her direction in life. Even when she was a child, she knew she wanted to be a broadcaster. She always talked about the first time she saw a black woman doing the news on TV. Sally-Ann was mesmerized. The woman was Trudy Daniels Haynes. Turned out she was a former classmate of my mom's at Howard University. Small world! From that moment Sally-Ann set her sights on being a TV journalist. Broadcasting was my sister's passion like sports was mine. As I prepared to graduate from high school, she planted the seed in me about becoming a journalist.

Now I had to focus on choosing a school that would help that seed grow. I thought I needed to go to a major university with an established communications department. The University of Tennessee was my first choice. It was an excellent school, not far from home, with a terrific women's basketball program. I requested a catalog from the university, but that was about it. I never told my parents or my high-school coach, Ann Logue, that I wanted to attend UT. It was one of the few times in my life that I didn't pursue something I wanted. Was I afraid to reach too high? Maybe I was. By the way, the UT women's basketball coach, Pat Summitt, has led the Lady Volunteers to eight national championships. No one—man or woman—has ever won more college basketball games than Pat.

I decided that I wanted to attend Louisiana State University in Baton Rouge. Like UT it was relatively close to home and a major university. I applied and was accepted—and was really elated when they offered me a basketball scholarship. Ann Logue offered to drive me to LSU for a visit. I was brimming with excitement as we made the 150-mile drive. LSU has a beautiful campus on the Mississippi River, but it's enormous. Two thousand acres, hundreds of buildings. It was a shock to my system. I was used to a small school in a small town. Walking around the huge, impersonal campus, I felt like I was shrinking. I couldn't picture myself there. I knew in my heart it wasn't for me.

I cried in the car heading back home. I'd already told my family and friends I was going to LSU, and I didn't want to disappoint them. I was ashamed of my reaction and embarrassed that Ann had taken the time to make this pointless trip. Most of all, I was scared that I was blowing my one big opportunity.

Then a small miracle happened. About fifty miles into our trip, we passed a sign for Southeastern

Louisiana University in Hammond, and on a whim we took the exit. It was love at first sight. I loved everything about the campus with its big oak trees and wide-open spaces. Hammond is the perfect small college town. It seemed just right for me.

It was so late in the school year that the only scholarship left was for tennis, but they offered it to me, promising I could also play basketball. I was in.

Southeastern didn't yet offer a degree in communications, but Coach Linda Puckett assured my parents and me that there would be a communications department by the time I was a senior. She encouraged me to see the advantages. No, Southeastern wasn't a big-time school like LSU, but I had an opportunity to grow with the university. My broadcast classes would not be overcrowded. Coach Puckett was right about that! In one broadcast class there were just two of us—Steve Zana and me. I was the reporter, and Steve was the cameraman. We'd go out in the field and put stories together. I can still remember the closing line for my report on the Ponchatoula Strawberry Festival: "A good time was had by all." Not exactly Emmy Award–winning material.

I was a good student, but during my first year of

college I felt like I was drifting. I was full of uncertainty, and that was a new feeling for me. I had always been so sure of where I was going, but I wasn't very comfortable in the broadcasting world. Was this going to be my life—standing with a microphone at local festivals and events? I kept trying to convince myself that broadcasting was right for me, but it wasn't working. By the end of the year I was convinced that I had made a mistake. I needed a new challenge. I told my parents that I had decided to drop out of school and become a pilot. Like my dad.

My parents were fantastic. They didn't panic, even though it was a goal of theirs to have all their kids graduate from college. My older siblings already had. I was the last one.

My dad said, "I'll make you a deal. I'll help you study for Officer Candidate School, because you have to be an officer to be a pilot. If you fail the test, you have to go back and finish at SLU." I agreed.

So my dad helped me study for the test. When he handed me the booklet (several inches thick) and I started paging through it, I thought, *Holy moly!* There were words that were the length of the page. I was in way over my head. I think my dad knew that, but he was nice enough not to rub it in. I took the test, but of course I didn't pass. Didn't even come close.

Back I went to SLU, and I was still not sure what direction I was heading in. That's when my big sis, Sally-Ann, stepped in.

Sally-Ann said, "You're missing it." She was exasperated.

I was clueless. "What?"

So she spelled it out for me. "You love sports, right?"

"Yes."

"And you like communications and broadcasting, right?"

"Yes."

"Sportscasting!" she announced.

I know I looked doubtful, but Sally-Ann gave me a pep talk. "You're just a little bit chicken because you don't see anybody like you doing it."

She was absolutely right. In the late 1970s there were very few women sportscasters, much less *black* women sportscasters. Who was I to think I could break such a daunting barrier? Still, I couldn't get the idea out of my head. It felt so right. That was my big fat "Aha!" moment. Now I had to make it a reality.

I bugged the local radio station in my college town,

WFPR, to hire me as its sports director. I was desperate to get any kind of practical experience. (Keep in mind, this was before internships were all the rage.) At first WFPR hired me as an assistant news director under the wonderful Mary Pirosko. She was patient with me, and she taught me as much as I was learning in the classroom, if not more. Mary is a dear friend to this day. I was lucky to have her as my guide.

I remember my first live newscast. I was scared out of my wits! The DJ, Roxanne, introduced me, and I delivered a brief news update. I wasn't half bad, despite the fact that I literally peed in my pants. I am not kidding you. I wet my pants and had to back out of the control room so nobody would notice.

I had other embarrassing moments on the air. I wrote most of my news scripts, but sometimes, if there was a late-breaking story, I would do what broadcasters call "rip and read." You rip the copy from the wire machine and read it cold on the air. One time I pronounced the word infamous as in-*famous*. The DJ I was working with was the station owner's son, Johnny Chauvin. When my newscast was over, he took me aside and politely corrected my error. I appreciated that he didn't make me feel stupid. I was doing a good enough job of that on my own.

He and the entire Chauvin family took me under their wing. WFPR was a rare breed—an honest-to-God family-owned station. "Big John" Chauvin had been in the broadcasting business for decades, and he and his wife, Frances, were pillars of the community. They had a large family, and everyone was involved at the station. They made me one of their own. They admired my determination. They even got a kick out of my having to ride a bicycle to work when I didn't have a car. To this day, Frances Chauvin, who is in her early eighties, visits me at the studio once a year, with her spectacular homemade pies in hand. My colleagues at ABC are very happy when she shows up.

I constantly hounded the Chauvins about moving from news to sports. Even though my heart wasn't in reporting the news I made sure I was always on time and did my absolute best. If I wasn't a good employee, how could I expect the Chauvins to honor my request? My patience and persistence paid off. In my junior year the Chauvins finally gave in and let me be the sports director. I could do play-by-play, host my own sports show—the works. I was thrilled. However, in exchange I had to give up my weekends and be a DJ. Did I mention that WFPR was a country music station? I can still remember my catchphrase: "WFPR, 14-country, your hometown country friend since 1947. This is Robin Rene here whicha [with you] on a Saturday night, playing the best in country music"—yee haw! You haven't lived until you scratch a little Merle Haggard on a 100-watt radio station.

It wasn't easy having a full load of classes, playing basketball, and working at the radio station. I had to be at the station by 6:00 a.m. I would do a couple of live sportscasts, then head back to campus in time for my 8:00 a.m. class. I had classes until noon, then went back to the station to tape my afternoon sports-casts and write copy for the disc jockeys. I usually had a couple of afternoon classes, then basketball practice from six to nine p.m. Then it was straight back to my dorm room to study. Having a hectic schedule like that certainly tried my patience. And let's face it, you don't have a whole lot of patience when you're in college.

I was in a hurry to get out of school and start my career. But believe it or not, my loaded schedule helped me focus. I know that a lot of people believe in multitasking. Not me. When you have so much on your plate, as many of us do, you can't do a good job on the next project until you successfully complete the one you're currently working on. When I was in class, I focused on the class. When I was at the radio station, it got my full attention. When I was on the basketball court, it was the only thing that mattered. I graduated with honors, cum laude, and was named Most Valuable Player of my basketball team my junior and senior years. Doing what you love makes everything possible.

Today, when I speak at commencements, I look out into the audience and I can see the panic in the graduates' eyes. I can almost hear their minds whirling— *What am I going to do? What am I going to do?* And I just want to reach out and hug them and say, "It's OK. A lot of people have felt just this way, and they worked it out. Don't panic—listen."

We all have an inner voice, and sometimes we ignore it, or it gets drowned out by all the noise of life. But I guarantee you that even today, I take time out to listen to mine. If you sit quietly and listen, you can hear it. And your inner voice will tell you what will really make you happy and fulfilled—what is truly in your heart. I have found it crucial in times of self-doubt to listen to that voice.

My Grandma Sally taught me how to listen to my inner voice. Every day she had "quiet time." No talking, no TV, no radio, no singing—just being alone with your thoughts and hearing the voice inside. As a child I was restless and I didn't like being quiet and sitting still. My sister Sally-Ann, my grandmother's namesake, took to it, though. She "got it" at a young age. To this day, Sally-Ann begins every morning with a period of quiet. It's as natural to her as breathing.

It took me longer to see the advantages, but eventually it became a habit, and now I appreciate quiet time. When I'm struggling with something, I always feel better and stronger after I've taken time to be still and listen. It's not just for the tough times either. I promise you, if you make it a regular part of your day, it will build your sense of self and bring you closer to the heart of what you really want in life.

For example, when I was debating whether I should leave sports for the anchor job at *GMA*, I listened to myself. My inner voice kept saying, *What are you scared about? Are you truly scared for yourself, or just scared of what people will think?* My inner voice came through loud and clear, asking the important questions, pushing me to examine my own heart and not be distracted by what others might say.

Sometimes it helps to visualize what you want. Actually close your eyes and see yourself in the position you want to be in. I used to do that when I bowled. I would step up to the lane, close my eyes, and envision exactly where I wanted the ball to go to knock down the pins. I would then open my eyes and attempt to duplicate what I had visualized moments earlier. I have used the same process when I've had to make a hard decision about which of two paths to take. Should I write this book? I actually visualized what it would look like well before I put anything down on paper.

And this doesn't just apply to those who are starting out. I've found that throughout my career I had to stay vigilant, listening to my inner voice.

You have to know who you are. It's more difficult than you think. I've worked with many people who just don't know who they are—don't know what they're passionate about. It's like they're on hold or in a fog.

If you're reading this and thinking you don't know yourself, I want to ask you something. Why? Have you just not taken the time to look inside? Is fear holding you back? Are you afraid you'll want something you don't think you can get? Whatever the reason, you have to get it straight, because if *you* don't know who you are and what you want, how can you walk into a job interview and expect a stranger to know?

Here's what you do. Begin by asking yourself a few simple questions: What do you like to do? What did you say as a kid when someone asked you what you wanted to be when you grew up? What are you happiest doing? What sparks your interest? What do you envision for yourself? I'm not just talking about career goals. Personal goals are just as important. Do you want to be in better shape? Do you want more out of your marriage or relationship? Do you want to own a house? Travel? Run for political office? Never forget that this is your one precious life. *Your* life. And you have the power to create your future. If you don't like the path you're taking, why in the world would you continue down that road?

Lastly, consider who you are and what works for *you*. We don't live in a one-size-fits-all world. You have to be able to see yourself fitting into a situation. Never let anyone else define happiness or success for you.

When I was working at WFPR during college, I once asked Mary Pirosko, "Why do you stay here?" Mary was so talented that I knew any station would consider itself lucky to have her. She was considered the radio equivalent to Walter Cronkite. That's how respected she was. But there she was in Hammond, Louisiana. She told me, "You don't necessarily have to be on a big stage to make a difference." I saw the truth to that, because Mary helped so many college kids like me. And she found it immensely fulfilling. She also helped establish quality programs and services for people with developmental disabilities, like her beloved son Stephen. Because of Mary, people with disabilities and challenges are valued, respected, and integral members of the Hammond community.

My sister Sally-Ann is incredibly popular in New Orleans. I sometimes say she's like the baby Oprah of her market. She has had many opportunities to go to larger markets. But that wasn't her dream; it was *my* dream. Sally-Ann's vision was to make a difference in

New Orleans and to raise her family. It was important to her that her children grow up in the place
where they were born. What has always impressed
me about Sally-Ann is how secure she is in her life's
path. I remember once being in her office and seeing
a letter on her desk from a TV station in San Fran-
cisco. A top-20 market was courting my big sis. I was
excited. Then I noticed that Sally-Ann had written
her grocery list on the back of the envelope. I couldn't
believe it. "What are you doing?" I practically shrieked
at her.

Sally-Ann just shrugged. "I've got to pick up gro-
ceries on my way home."

I bombarded her with questions: Had she written
back? Had she talked to them? Was she considering it?

She just laughed. "Robin," she said, "you know I
love New Orleans. I'm not leaving. It's my home."

For me, "home" could encompass the world. For
Sally-Ann, home is New Orleans. We each made our
choices according to our different dreams.

My sister Dorothy has numerous talents. She's the
one who makes most of my necklaces that *GMA*
viewers rave about. And, boy, can Dorothy sing! In
fact, in 1976 she was an All-American singer and

performed that summer as part of Disney World's Bicentennial Celebration.

Dorothy had dreams of performing on the big stage one day. But she opted for getting married right after college and starting a family. She fulfills her artistic needs by singing in the church choir and performing in local theatre productions. And her little sister is there in the front row, cheering her on.

Life is about making choices. That's pretty much what it boils down to. My professional choices have meant that I don't have the kind of family life Sally Ann and Dorothy have. But I know what works for me. You have to find that for yourself.

Recently, I had a phone conversation with an intern at ESPN. She was a bright young woman, full of passion for sportscasting. She'd be graduating from college the following year, and she wanted to pick my brain about how she could be successful. I like to talk to young people and give them advice. I always remember the generous people who did the same for me. This young woman was extremely careful about getting down every word I said. She was sitting at her computer on the other end of the line, and I could hear her typing furiously as I answered her questions. I started laughing as I realized that she was treating the conversation like manna from heaven. She thought if only she could capture the exact recipe for broadcasting success, she'd have it made.

"Look, sweetheart," I said warmly, "it's really great that you're getting all of this input. It's important to do that. But you have to personalize it. You can talk to ten different people and hear ten different ways to get where you want to go. Only you know what is going to work for you, so I want you to think about that. Don't sell yourself short. When it comes to your dream and your goal and your livelihood, don't leave it up to anybody else."

Everyone can be a success in life if they are doing what they love. There is a tendency to measure our success by what others do. I get frustrated when I hear women putting other women down because they've made different choices. If you're true to yourself, you're doing the right thing. There is no "wrong."

I'd like to help women get past their insecurities. We all have different strengths and weaknesses. Each of us has unique, wonderful gifts to offer. Please don't lose the opportunity to be *you*.

3. If at First You Don't Succeed, Dive Back In

Do you know how many calls, letters, and e-mails I receive from college students who want to be broadcasters? Only a very small percentage of them will go on to achieve their goal. Not because they lack talent or potential, but because they won't have the stamina to stick it out when they run into obstacles.

Sometimes when I'm advising a young woman about breaking into sportscasting, she'll have it in her head that she can bypass all that grueling "getting experience" business and go straight to the top. When I ask her for a plan, she'll say something like, "Well, I want to host the NBA show *Inside Stuff*."

I'll press, "But in the meantime . . ."

"No, now."

"Now?" I'll look at this fresh-faced kid and my heart will sink as she explains that she wants her first job to be broadcasting for the NBA.

Sometimes I'll say, "Do you want to know what *my* first job was?"—all ready to tell her how I climbed up from the bottom, making $5.50 an hour. But her eyes are already glazing over. She doesn't want to hear it. She wants to be a superstar right now.

I was the only one in my graduating class to get a job in TV. Was it because I was the smartest? Hardly. It was because I was patient and persistent. I flooded TV stations around the country with my résumé tape. When I asked my classmates where they were sending their résumés, they said places like New York, Chicago, Los Angeles—top TV markets. When they asked me where I had sent my tapes, I told them Timbuktu. I wanted a job!

My first job out of college was as a part-time sports anchor at a local TV station, in Hattiesburg, Mississippi, about an hour and a half drive from Pass Christian. Sally-Ann had once worked for the station, and she put in a good word for me. I remember her telling me, "I can open a door for you, but you have to be the one to keep it open and step through it." My salary was a whopping $5.50 an hour for thirty hours a week. But I chose this part-time job over a more lucrative full-time job as a news anchor and reporter with WLOX in Biloxi. Most broadcast majors would have jumped at a news anchor job, but I knew myself and what I wanted by then. I was a sportscaster, and my goal was to eventually become a network sportscaster. So the part-time job made sense to me as a step along the path I had set for myself.

My parents were supportive, but I knew they would have preferred that I take the full-time job. My friends didn't understand my decision. After all, wasn't the objective of going to college to land a higher-paying job? Maybe for some, but not for me. I truly wanted to follow my passion and my heart. And that was sports—pure and simple. Money has never motivated me. As you will see, I often took less money for a job I thought would lead me to my ultimate goal—network sportscaster. I was single-minded—my parents would say *stubborn*. But I just knew beyond a shadow of a doubt that I would find joy there.

I always try to make my job choices for the right reasons—that is, not for the money or the glory, but because whatever I'm doing will make me happy. I believe that a certain karma happens when you follow the direction your heart takes you.

In this case, it turned out to be the right decision. Nine months into the job in Hattiesburg, WLOX had an opening in their sports department and they came right to me. They knew I had taken less money to be in sports. They wanted someone with that kind of passion on their sports staff.

I thoroughly enjoyed being a sportscaster at WLOX. It was the station I grew up watching on the Mississippi Gulf Coast. It was a jewel. Not a top market, but an absolute wonder, with a talented staff. (In 2005, during Hurricane Katrina, the professionals at WLOX really pulled together. They remained on the air the whole time. Many of the staff had lost their homes, but they selflessly put their feelings aside and stayed with the story.)

When I joined WLOX, Dave Vincent was the news director, and he still is. Dave taught me so much about journalism. His criticism was always constructive. He didn't hesitate to tell me what I was doing wrong, then patiently show me how to do it the right way. I was happy—boy, was I happy. My family and friends surrounded me. I even lived back at home with my folks for a while. Then I moved into a brand-new apartment and bought myself a nice new car. I thought I was all that and a bag of chips. I was enjoying covering teams and coaches I had once played against. Even though I was different from most sportscasters, viewers didn't make me feel that way. Oh, sure, some of them gave me a hard time, but it was usually for something I did or said, not for who I was. People would sound off if they thought I was favoring one team over another, or if they didn't like what I was wearing. But only a very few had a problem with my gender or my race. My parents were well respected on the Coast, and I was their baby girl. Plus my sports knowledge was rarely challenged because I was a local sports standout. And I did my homework. I thoroughly researched stories I was assigned. Plus I read at least three newspapers a day as well as numerous sports magazines.

I loved everything about being a sports journalist. It was a thrill to attend the games, capture the excitement on tape, then write a story that would make viewers feel as if they were sitting on the sidelines. It was a challenge to find new ways of covering a story. But the truth is I was really in my comfort zone. In fact, I was so comfortable, I started losing sight of the big picture—which for me was becoming a network sportscaster. My wake-up call came when WLOX offered me the primetime news anchor position. It was a big promotion for a lot more money, but I knew in my heart that it would not make me happy. I politely declined their generous offer. It was time to move to a bigger TV market.

I started sending my tapes to TV stations in the Southeast. All I wanted was an interview. I felt that if I could just get in the door, I could sell them on what an asset I'd be to their station. But it seemed that as fast as I sent my tapes out, they were coming right back to me stamped REJECT. OK, they didn't really stamp the word "reject" on them, but it sure felt that way. Those tapes came back so fast, I couldn't believe they'd even been opened. I kept thinking, couldn't they just keep the tape for a couple of weeks and make it look like they were considering me? I couldn't get an interview anywhere. I hounded one news director in Houston, Texas—mustering all of my courage to make the calls.

At least he'd talk to me. He was encouraging, but he never gave me an interview or offered me a job. I was frustrated, and I began to feel defeated. It's so easy for those doubts to sneak in. They only need the tiniest little opening. I started thinking maybe I wasn't so good after all. Maybe I should take the news anchor job at WLOX and be satisfied.

Then I realized that I was letting others tell me what I could and could not do, and I was determined not to let that happen. Instead, I got creative. I kept being told by news directors that they didn't have it in their budgets to fly me in for an interview. So I put on my thinking cap. My parents were traveling a great deal for our church at the time, so I asked them to give me advance notice of their trips. Then I'd send my tape and résumé to all the TV stations in that area. I wouldn't ask for a job, but just for a critique of my tape. That way, they wouldn't feel any pressure. Then I would tell them I was going to be in their area and would welcome the opportunity to come by the station. It wouldn't cost them a nickel. Wouldn't cost me anything either, since I would hitch a ride with my folks and stay in their hotel room.

My creativity finally paid off. My parents were going to Opryland for a church meeting. Nashville was close by, so I arranged an interview with Alan Griggs, the news director at WSMV in Nashville, and drove up with my parents. WSMV was an impressive station. It had won many prestigious Peabody Awards. I was so glad I arranged the interview. Alan and I hit it off instantly. He told me to stay in touch until he had an opening on his staff. He wasn't giving me the runaround. He really meant it.

A few months later, Alan called to say there was an opening at WSMV for a lifestyle reporter.

"Uh . . . lifestyle?" I was disappointed. It wasn't what I was looking for. I couldn't see myself doing fashion and cooking segments.

Alan heard my dismay and quickly explained that it was just a bookkeeping thing. Technically, I'd be listed as a lifestyle reporter, but in reality I'd be in the sports department. I trusted him, and he was true to his word. Even the pretense of being a lifestyle reporter didn't last long. I quickly became a full-fledged member of the WSMV sports team, reporting on the Vanderbilt University Commodores and the University of Tennessee Volunteers.

I especially enjoyed anchoring, but I only had a chance to fill in occasionally for the regular anchors. I was very excited the first time I subbed for the weekday sports anchor, Rudy Kalis. I wanted to make sure that my sportscast was perfect and memorable. It was memorable all right!

The station was located in a large rambling two-story building. The sports office was upstairs at one end, and the studio was downstairs at the other end. I made sure I was at the studio in plenty of time. The news anchor said, "Robin Roberts will have the sports for us right after these messages." We went to a two-minute commercial break and I calmly took my seat next to the news anchor. I was ready, with time to spare. Just then the director came on the intercom in a panic. He didn't have my sports tapes. I'd left them on my desk in the sports office! I jumped up and ran as fast as I could down the long hallway and up the stairs to my office. I grabbed the tapes and raced back downstairs to the control room, handed the tapes to the director, and ran back to the studio. I got back in place on the set with only seconds to spare. The news anchor introduced me. I opened my mouth to speak, and nothing came out. I was completely winded. My eyes started watering; I didn't know what to do. When I was finally able to catch my breath, I told the audience what had happened during the commercial break. I started laughing, and so did everyone in the studio. I thought it was the end of my career in Nashville. But the phone lines lit up—I was a hit! Viewers thought it was hilarious, and more importantly, they appreciated how I had found humor in a potentially embarrassing situation.

In Nashville I learned to be versatile, and to make the most of every opportunity. It's not always obvious how one thing is going to lead to another, but sometimes you have to go with the flow. Often the most unlikely situation gives you the biggest boost.

There was a tremendously popular morning show at WSMV called the *Ralph Emery Show*. Ralph Emery was like the Johnny Carson of country music. His show was on every weekday morning from five to seven. It was similar to a variety show. Up-and-coming country music stars would perform. Many of the commercials were done live in the studio, starring the local retailers themselves. These auto dealers, florists, and furniture-store owners were like minimedia stars. There was even a live studio audience.

Two elderly sisters named Maude and Dorothy were in the audience every day. The show may sound corny, but it was an institution in Nashville. Everybody watched it.

Ralph was a big sports fan, so Alan approached him about my becoming the sports director for the show. Ralph agreed, and I wrote, produced, and anchored two sportscasts every morning. We even had "sporting events" on the show, such as paddleboat races and outhouse races. (Don't ask!) We'd compete against the sales staff and the local retailers. One year my team won the paddleboat race. I immediately checked to see if I could turn pro. Being on the *Ralph Emery Show* was an unexpected bonus. It helped me hone my anchoring skills, and it taught me invaluable lessons about live television that I use to this day: How to think quickly on your feet. How to effortlessly transition from one subject to the next. And most importantly, how to not take yourself too seriously. Because, my friends, anything can happen on *live* television.

I always kind of chuckle when young people say they want to know my formula for success and want to duplicate what I did every step of the way. It doesn't work like that. Life is more serendipitous. You never know which experiences are going to be of value. I don't think someone planning a career at ESPN or *Good Morning America* would necessarily say, "I'll start with the *Ralph Emery Show*. Those paddleboat races will get me where I want to go." But it happened that way for me. You've got to leave yourself open to the hidden opportunities of life.

I had a lot of success in Nashville. WSMV was consistently number one in the ratings, and the *Nashville Scene*, a local paper, named me Sportscaster of the Year during my time there. After two years, stations in bigger cities began showing interest in me. In 1987, I was thrilled to receive an offer from WAGA in Atlanta to be a sports reporter. It would give me an opportunity to cover pro teams for the first time—the Falcons, the Braves, and the Hawks. As I considered the move, I received a call from ESPN. They wanted me to fly up to Bristol, Connecticut, for an interview. That was a heady moment. I was just four years out of college, and the worldwide leader in sports wanted to meet *me*. It's safe to say I was a wee bit excited. Who am I kidding? I went bonkers! Working at ESPN had been a dream of mine since I had taken my hairbrush (microphone) to interview teammates in college. Oh, they loved me for doing that.

My flight to ESPN was delayed several hours, and it was well after midnight by the time I reached my hotel. The clerk at the front desk didn't even look up as I came through the door. He just said in a bored voice, "Call your mother." Here I was, twenty-six years old, about to meet with ESPN, but my mother was back home worried about me because I hadn't called. It was a little embarrassing, but I have to say I felt a warm glow. I don't think you ever get too old to not appreciate a long-distance hug from Mom.

My interviews with the ESPN executives went well. I also met *SportsCenter* anchors, including the wildly popular Chris Berman and Dan Patrick. At first it seemed like a dream come true. But the network was still very young at the time, and they couldn't tell me exactly what my duties would be. It would be a leap of faith on both of our parts if I accepted a position there.

With two good offers on the table, I had a decision to make. Many people thought I should take the ESPN job. After all, wasn't my goal to be a network sportscaster? But I knew myself. I thought I needed more experience to have any real staying power at ESPN. I'd never even covered pro teams. I didn't want to be the answer to a trivia question: "What woman was hired by ESPN in 1987 and fired a year later?"

So I took the job in Atlanta. It was the right decision, professionally and personally. Atlanta is an amazing city, with a great energy and vibe. I loved it there, and I traveled with Atlanta's NBA team, the Hawks. I got to know players like Dominique Wilkins and Doc Rivers, and I was gratified to earn their respect. Head coach Mike Fratello always treated me fairly—that is, he treated me the same as all the male reporters covering the Hawks.

I also became a radio personality in Atlanta, working for V-103, the top-rated urban contemporary station. I have to say there are a lot of advantages to radio. People *listen* to you. They're not distracted by your hair and clothes—and *you're* not distracted by your hair and clothes. I was part of the morning show (of course, it was a morning show) hosted by Mike Roberts. I had a couple of sportscasts on the show, but I was more like Mike's cohost. He was a phenomenal host and extremely popular. All the major stars who came to town visited us in the studio. I met and interviewed Will Smith, Smokey Robinson, Deion Sanders—the list went on and on. I was living happily ever after in Atlanta—or so I thought. I finally felt that all of my persistence and hard work was paying off.

I know what it's like to want something right away. Maybe you've reached the difficult decision to make a change in your life, and you're eager to see the results now. You become frustrated if things don't go according to your time frame. When this happens to me—and it does—I just say to myself, "God's delays are not His denials." He has put me in situations or allowed situations to happen—many times painful. Like not getting a job I thought I was perfect for. Or negative things being written about me in the paper. And the most painful, my father's unexpected death. But that is how I grew.

Don't ever let anyone tell you that you can't do something. More importantly, never tell yourself that. At times it may take you longer than you like to get where you want to go. But if you're patient and persistent, you *will* get there.

Every action you take is one step closer to your goal—even if it's just a baby step. I remember when I was looking for jobs, I had to swallow my dread and just make the calls. It was so hard to gear myself up. But I always felt better and more confident once I picked up the phone and did it. Even if the person didn't take the call or was dismissive, it felt like a small victory that I'd been brave enough to dial the number. If you look for those daily victories, even the rejections can make you stronger.

Life isn't all about rejection, of course, and I have often reflected on the fact that my ability to pursue my dreams depended in large part on the willingness of others to hold the door open for me and let me walk through. I was black, I was Southern, and I was a woman in what was traditionally a man's world. I knew that determination alone would not get me in. I had to ask for help and to seek out mentors. I got pretty good at it too. To this day, I am amazed when I think about the people who helped me, and I've done my best to do the same for the young people coming up.

None of us gets there on our own. I'll never forget the time I lost sight of that for a moment. Thankfully, my mother was there to remind me. In the early 1990s, I gave a commencement speech at the University of Southern Mississippi. My mother was in the audience. In my speech I talked about the things I had done, what I had learned, how I'd coped with adversity, and the importance of following your passion.

After the speech, I noticed that my mother was very quiet. I finally said, "What's the problem?"

She just looked at me, then she said, "Do you know how many people have helped you? When you were standing up there, it wasn't just you. It was your teachers, your coaches, your mentors like the Chauvins, Dave Vincent, John Walsh, and so many others."

I listened to her words and I felt ashamed. Oh, my God, she was so right. Why didn't I acknowledge them? And I realized that it wasn't just the speech. I hadn't fully acknowledged the debt of gratitude I owed to others. It was one of the few times my mother had ever expressed disappointment in me. Her words stung, but they were true.

My mother has frequently spoken with gratitude and reverence of the woman who made the biggest difference in *her* life. It was her second-grade teacher, Wilma Schnegg-Merold. She was widowed young and never had children of her own, but she poured her heart into helping an entire generation of children. Ms. Schnegg-Merold saw something special in the bright little girl Lucimarian, and she decided on her own to become Mom's unofficial counselor. She advised her all the way through high school, and she was determined that my mother was going to college. She envisioned a life for her beyond her own expectations, and she set out to make it happen. She helped Mom get a scholarship to Howard University, and when the money ran out in her junior year, she organized a recital to raise the cash. Mom once said, "Her legacy to me is the awareness that you're always a little bit better and a little bit stronger than you think you are."

We need one another. If you scratch the surface of a successful person, you will see the generosity and sacrifice of others that went into making it happen. I am extremely touched by the selflessness of so many professional broadcast journalists—even those who were my competitors—in helping me reach my goals. Believe me, it is an impressive thing to work with people who are solely focused on the excellence of the program, and aren't threatened by a new face. I can't tell you how much I appreciated the openheartedness of Diane Sawyer and Charlie Gibson when I joined them as coanchor of *Good Morning America*. Everyone had warned me that the world of national morning television was a dog-eat-dog world. I found just the opposite.

It is important to acknowledge those who help you. Equally important is reaching a hand back to lift up and support those who are following behind. You can make the legacy of generosity *more* generosity.

4. Never Play the Race, Gender, or Any Other Card

Many of us are quick to think the worst of people—and to assume they think the worst of us. That's exhausting. It also gets in the way. When you believe you can't succeed because other people won't let you, it's like rolling a big boulder into the center of your path.

I remember the first (and what turned out to be the only) time I complained to my parents, "I know I didn't get that job because I'm a black woman." They were having none of it. They sat me down, looked me square in the eyes, and said, "Did you stop to think that maybe you didn't get the job because you're not good enough yet?" Ouch! Boy, does the truth hurt, especially when it comes from the two people who love you the most.

People often ask me, "What was it like growing up as a black person in Mississippi?" I think our experience was somewhat different from that of many other black families. We'd traveled around the world. We'd lived among other cultures. Our view wasn't so black and white. When we moved to Mississippi, we didn't know we weren't supposed to do certain things, and sometimes people were shocked. They'd say, "What's with those Roberts kids?"

Our parents shielded us in many ways. Not that we didn't experience some harsh realities. But they always put the focus on what we could do. They expected us to better ourselves. No excuses accepted. The only time I can remember them cautioning me was when I was on a traveling bowling team. This was the early 1970s, and we were going to the northern part of Mississippi, around Jackson. At that time, it could get a little dicey for blacks in that area. My parents sat me down and they said, "Honey, if you're out with your team and it starts to get a little dark, don't run. Take our word for it. Just walk briskly."

"Uh, OK." I didn't know what they were talking about, but I agreed. I guess they were afraid someone would see a black girl running and think she was running away from trouble.

Another reason Dad and Mom were different was that they were from New Jersey and Ohio. It was a culture shock to them when they first lived in the South early in Dad's career. They'd never seen separate entrances or water fountains for blacks and whites. My mom loves to tell the story of when she took my brother, Lawrence (we call him Butch), to shop at Montgomery Fair—an Alabama department store where, incidentally, Rosa Parks worked as a seamstress. This was during the Tuskegee Boycott, when blacks boycotted Tuskegee merchants after being denied the right to vote in city elections. They drove forty miles to Montgomery to do their shopping. It was the first time Butch had ever seen separate water fountains—one labeled WHITE, and one labeled COLORED. He excitedly ran up to the COLORED fountain, but he walked away disappointed. He sulked. "That's just plain ol' water," he complained. "It isn't colored."

My mother always stressed that we were to never

use race as an excuse. To always look first to ourselves and address the things we needed to improve. It was the way her mother raised her, and she passed it on to us.

Mom told us of the time she tried out for a high school regional choir. It was a very big deal. She had a beautiful singing voice, and all her friends told her she'd be chosen. But when the names were posted on the bulletin board, her name was not there. She was irate that she'd been passed over because she was black. It was so unfair. But when she complained to her mother, her mother said, "Well, maybe you didn't blend. Maybe your voice is more of a solo voice, and the choir director was looking for someone who could blend in."

My mother wasn't buying it. She said, "No, I know how to blend."

And her mother said, "Well, maybe they were looking for a soprano and you sang alto."

And my mother said, "No, during the tryouts, first I sang alto, and then I sang soprano."

And her mother said, "Well, maybe you were just a little too show-offy."

My mother always recounted that incident. "I

knew it was because I was black," she said. "But my mother just wouldn't let me say that." It was many years later that my mom learned her mother went to the school and voiced her concern. The principal talked to the choir director. My mom recalled that suddenly the choir director did make a point to give her the same opportunities as her classmates. Grandma Sally didn't want my mom to get trapped in a victim mentality, because she saw the value of focusing on your personal excellence. And Mom passed the same mentality on to her children.

When it came to self-determination, my parents were amazing role models for their children and others. They spent their whole lives breaking down barriers, but they did it quietly. They never got on a soapbox. They just kept pressing against the barriers until they fell away.

In the Air Force, my dad's division, the all-black Tuskegee Airmen, was segregated from the white divisions in the early days. And my dad wasn't always treated with the respect he was due. Once, after serving in Japan, he was transferred to an Air Force base outside of Dallas. My parents arrived about nine p.m., assuming there would be accommodations for them. They were stopped at the gate to the base, and the guard said, "You'll have to go into Dallas. There is no housing available for you." And he was very pointed when he said "*for you.*"

My parents drove into Dallas and had no luck finding lodging. Finally, a black proprietor took pity on them and said, "I do have one place . . ." It was a room in a brothel. The doorbell rang all night.

Things actually got worse, not better. Often there were no lodgings on base for black families. My mother got used to the way the other officers' wives looked at her when she showed up at their coffee gatherings. They couldn't believe a black woman belonged in a group of officers' wives. She always made it a point to go to the coffees, though. Welcome or not, in her quiet way she asserted her rights and her dignity. That's probably why many years later my mom became president of the Officers Wives' Club. And she never said a word about it.

It must have been very painful, but my parents were never bitter. I'm sure they must have complained at times. But they never let their children see their frustration. They were extremely patriotic. They believed that they could succeed because that's what America was all about. And they made it happen, in spite of the barriers.

People have said that I'm a trailblazer, but believe me, the path was already cleared of the heaviest brush by my parents and others of their generation before I ever set foot on it.

I've had many occasions during my career to recall my parents' determination and openheartedness in the face of resistance. As an aspiring sportscaster, my gender was often a much bigger barrier than my race. I knew it wouldn't be an easy road. Women sportscasters were few and far between. The only black woman I saw was Jayne Kennedy, who was briefly on the CBS show *NFL Today*. She was a former beauty queen, just like Phyllis George, who also appeared on that show. Both women were gorgeous and talented. But they weren't necessarily hired for their sports knowledge. I greatly admired them. However, my strength was knowing sports. It was certainly not my looks!

Back in the early 1980s, when I was just starting my career, there was a lot of controversy about women sports reporters entering men's locker rooms, the traditional settings for postgame interviews. Believe me, I hated going in there too. I wasn't fighting for equal access to the locker room. I was fighting for equal access to the athlete who just happened to be in the locker room.

In 1988, when I went to work for WAGA in Atlanta, my first major assignment was covering the University of Georgia in the Southeastern Conference Men's Basketball Tournament. The university, like so many at the time, had a policy of not allowing women reporters in the locker room. If a woman wanted an interview with a particular athlete, she had to put in a request and the athlete would be brought to an interview room. It wasn't an ideal situation, but I always played by the rules, so I put in my request and waited patiently with my cameraman.

While I was waiting, I watched the male reporters from competing Atlanta TV stations leaving the locker room with their taped interviews in hand. We all had a deadline to file our stories for the eleven o'clock nightly news. My competitors were heading back to their stations while I was still waiting for my interviews. I did a slow burn, and finally I'd had enough. I turned to my cameraman and said, "We're going in!"

Just as I lowered my shoulder to charge into the locker room, a university official stopped me. I demanded to speak to the star of the game immediately. The official ran into the locker room, and the next thing I knew I was talking to a player dripping wet in the hallway. He had literally been pulled out of the shower. Thankfully, he'd stopped long enough to wrap himself in a towel before answering my questions. But it was a suspiciously *small* towel.

Was I trying to be a jerk? No, I was trying to keep my job. Imagine if my boss was watching all the newscasts that evening and he saw that our station was the only one without an interview with the star of the game. He would call the station and ask what happened. If he was told, "We sent Robin to cover the game, but she couldn't get into the locker room," do you think I would have had a job for very long?

Believe it or not, this inequity did not make me angry. It just made me get creative. I developed an understanding with the teams I covered on a regular basis. If I was working on a feature story that didn't have a particular deadline, I would interview players after practice on the court and not in the locker room. If I was covering a game and had a deadline, I was allowed equal access to the athletes so I could do my job just like everybody else. But I always said a Hail Mary before I went into the locker room—and I'm not even Catholic.

Interviewing players in the locker room after a game is part of the lore of sports—the immediacy, the emotion. But personally, I think we could do without it. If you want immediacy, set aside a space for players to talk to reporters right after the game, before they hit the showers. It's not comfortable for anyone. Male reporters don't like it either, and neither do the players. Michael Jordan made a point of never undressing as long as reporters were in the locker room.

Athletes and coaches have always treated me with respect, and vice versa. Part of it was that they just wanted to be treated fairly by the media, and they could sense that's all I wanted too—to be treated fairly. Plus my passion for sports was obvious, and they appreciated that. I truly believe that people are drawn to those who are passionate about their work. Think about it. Isn't it great when you see somebody who obviously loves his or her job? It sure puts a smile on *my* face to see it.

It wasn't only the professionals whose respect I had to earn. It was the public, too. When I started as a sportscaster in Nashville, they didn't know me from Adam's house cat. I was just this woman who thought she could do a man's job. Those were the days when people would debate whether a woman was really capable of doing play-by-play. Before I started in Nashville, a local paper published a feature on me, so people knew I was coming. Not everyone was thrilled.

My first day on the job, before I'd even been on the air, my phone rang. The voice on the other end was gruff. He sounded like an older gentleman. "I want to speak with Robin Roberts," he demanded.

"This is she," I said cautiously.

"I don't like you." That's what he said. *I-don't-like-you.*

I was a bit indignant. "What do you mean, you don't like me? I haven't done anything yet." Yes, I was a bit defensive.

He said, "I don't like women in sports." And then he launched into a tirade about how women had to ruin everything, and why did we have to get into sports, anyway, and on and on. I just listened until he ran out of steam, and then I said, as calmly as I could, "Look, I'll tell you what. Give me six months. Watch my reports. Then call me back." I was asking for a chance, a fair shot.

Three months later, he was back on the phone: "Is this Robin Roberts?" Uh-oh! I knew that voice.

"Yes," I said, waiting for the tirade.

"Aw," he said, somewhat reluctantly, "I guess you're all right."

It wasn't exactly a ringing endorsement, but he had given me a chance and that's all I wanted.

Don't let others define you or dictate your attitude. At the same time, don't assume that if you don't get that job or opportunity, it's because someone has it in for you or has a prejudice against you. Give them the benefit of the doubt. Chances are, they deserve it. I've found that most people in positions of power and influence want to help others achieve, and the public is amazingly openhearted.

You cannot control what other people say or do, or how they think. You only have control over what *you* say or do, and how *you* think. Never was this clearer to me than when I worked in Atlanta.

I was featured in a major newspaper article. It was a flattering story, praising my work at a local TV station. The reporter could not have been more complimentary. But in the article she referred to me as a "two-fer." I had no idea what that meant. I actually had to call my mother and ask her. She said, "Robin, it means you are a double minority. You're a woman and you're black."

Oh. That's right. I remembered that discussion. The interview had been very positive, and I was feeling good. At one point the reporter slipped in a remark, saying that my boss could check off two boxes when it came to being an equal opportunity employer. In a sense she was implying that being a black woman helped me get the job. Then she asked a leading question like, "Isn't that true?" and I just went with it. I kind of nodded agreeably, and said, "Yeah, I guess it is." What in the heck was I thinking?

The story got picked up by the Associated Press and ran all over the country, including New Orleans, where Sally-Ann's husband, Willie, saw it. My brother-in-law was livid! Not at the reporter—at me. He called me up and started right in on me: "You know how hard you've worked to be where you are. Nothing has ever been handed to you. If other people want to say you got the job because of the color of your skin, let them. But don't let me ever hear *you* say it, because it's not true."

Willie was right, and his words stayed with me. I realized how easily I could slip into a mentality of not feeling I deserved the best. I was so happy to be working as a sportscaster in a major market that I tried to justify it in my own mind.

The lesson was well learned, just in time for ESPN to come calling again. It had been two years since we'd last met. I had grown, and so had ESPN. I interviewed with John Walsh, the managing editor of *SportsCenter.* John was relatively new to ESPN. He had a print background, having been managing editor of *U.S. News & World Report* and *Rolling Stone* magazines. I was impressed with the interview. John had a definite vision for the program, for the network, and for me. His enthusiasm was contagious.

I left the interview feeling exhilarated but, again, I was torn. I loved my life in Atlanta. I would also have to take a pay cut—my combined salary working for the TV and radio stations was substantial. I realized that if I moved to Connecticut, I would be living on the East Coast for the first time in my life—far away from my friends and family. That would be very difficult. But John, who is one of the most brilliant minds and astounding human beings I have ever met in my life, encouraged me. He allowed me to see that I could flourish at ESPN.

Ironically, one of the first big stories I did at ESPN was about Lisa Olson, a sports reporter for the *Boston Herald*, who was involved in a highly publicized locker-room incident. By 1990, women reporters were generally allowed equal access, but as Lisa learned, changing the rules doesn't necessarily mean changing people's minds and hearts. After an NFL game, while Lisa was conducting interviews in the New England Patriots locker room, a group of team members surrounded her, taunting her and shouting vulgarities. It was not only intimidating, but also deeply humiliating. When the incident came to light, it was front-page news all over the country. The players were fined, and the general manager was fired for trying to cover up the story. It should have ended there, but instead, Lisa's life became a nightmare. She received death threats ("Leave Boston or die"), her tires were slashed, her apartment was vandalized, and her mail was filled with angry, obscene letters. It got so bad that Lisa was transferred out of the country—all the way to Sydney, Australia. Eventually, she returned to the States as a sports reporter for the New York *Daily News*. She's tough. But her experience in Boston made a lot of people sit up and pay attention. It takes generations to break down the walls of bias that are ingrained in the culture. Thanks to ESPN and other pioneers in promoting women sportscasters and reporters, we've come a long way.

We're not there yet, but I see the signs pointing in that direction. Each generation is more open. When I was at ESPN and was asked to speak to fourth-graders at a school in Norwalk, Connecticut, the teacher who invited me was extremely enthusiastic. In fact, he was a little bit over the top. He introduced me to the kids like he was pointing out some rare and awesome species: "LOOK, KIDS, A BLACK WOMAN, AND SHE'S A SPORTSCASTER. AMAZING!"

When I got to the question-and-answer period, a little boy raised his hand.

He said, "I like you and I think you're good. I don't care if you're a girl."

I grinned at him, and said, "Well, we'll be looking forward to your getting older when you can hire people." And that's the point. These kids naturally see women in the sports world and in other professions that were once closed to them, and when they grow up it will be no big deal for them to work alongside women. Or to see them on TV in prominent positions.

I'll tell you one thing. I know that whatever goals we achieve, individually and collectively, it will not happen through incivility. If you have to cut someone else down to build yourself up, it's not a clean win. Even in the worst of times, a positive attitude and an open spirit will get you further than anger and resentment.

I remember one time seeing the phenomenal poet Maya Angelou on *The Oprah Winfrey Show*. Oprah was talking to her good friend and mentor about growing older. Dr. Angelou said some inspirational things that I will never forget. She said: "I've learned that whenever I decide something with an open heart, I usually make the right decision. I've learned even when I have pains, I don't have to be one. I've learned that every day you should reach out and touch someone. People love a warm hug, or just a friendly pat on the back."

I really want you to think about this last thing Dr. Angelou said: "I've learned that people will forget what you said, people will forget what you did, but people will never forget how you made them feel."

You know how it is when you meet someone and later you can't remember what that person said, but you do remember the good feeling you had after you walked away from them? Strive to be the kind of person who elicits that feeling in others.

5. Venture Outside Your Comfort Zone

I loved ESPN. I've always said, I was at ESPN for fifteen years and I never worked a single day. It didn't feel like work. How many people can claim that?

John Walsh was one of the biggest sports fans I'd ever met—and that's saying a lot! He could barely sit still he was so passionate. Being at ESPN was a dream come true for him. We hit it off because he saw the same passion in me.

John and I had something else in common—our curiosity. We both asked questions, challenged ourselves, wondered, "What would happen if . . . ?" and

"What if we did this?" It was an extremely creative environment.

Being a *SportsCenter* anchor was a wonderful opportunity, but I was always reaching for more. I had been at ESPN just a few months when I learned that there was an opening on one of the network's premier shows, *NFL PrimeTime*, hosted by Chris Berman. Chris was by far the most popular personality at ESPN—and he still is to this day. He and the much-respected Bob Ley have been at ESPN since the very beginning. The first time I did the six p.m. *Sports-Center* (after a month on the overnight shift), Chris was my coanchor. I sensed that all the male viewers would take their cue from Chris. If he liked me, they would like me. Chris treated me with respect, both on and off the air, and his attitude helped me get accepted by others.

John Walsh had already approached me about becoming the host of a new show, *Sunday SportsDay*. John wanted the program to be almost like reading the Sunday paper. Of course, we'd have highlights, but the show would have a nice, relaxing pace to it. I would host a portion of the show from ESPN headquarters in Bristol, and my cohost in New York would be none other than the legendary Dick Schaap.

I walked into John's office and told him how much I appreciated the opportunity to host *Sunday Sports-Day*. Then I asked him about the opening on *NFL PrimeTime*, which aired Sunday nights after the football games. When he told me the position was still open, I burst out that I wanted that job too.

Now, John could have said, "Whoa! You've only been here a few months. Don't push your luck." Instead, he said he'd think about it.

After I left John's office I wondered if I'd gone too far. Asked for too much. But almost immediately I realized how at peace I was for having had the nerve to walk in and make that request. I knew that wanting the job and not asking for it would have been more painful than being turned down.

At the end of the week John called me back into his office and said, "I'm going to take you up on your offer." The *PrimeTime* job was mine! Would John have offered me that plum assignment had I not had the nerve to ask? Probably not. I worked with Chris ("Boomer") Berman and Tom ("TJ") Jackson for six years on *NFL PrimeTime*. TJ was a former NFL standout for the Denver Broncos. He's a big guy with an even bigger heart. Boomer, TJ, and Rockin' Robin. It was a wonderful time. I just loved it. But don't think I wasn't aware that I constantly had to prove myself to viewers, who were mostly male. I was always on my toes, because the slightest slip could be an indictment on women sportscasters. I knew that if Chris Berman were to jokingly say "innings" instead of "quarters," people would laugh and say, "Oh, that Boomer." But if I were to do the same thing, they'd be crying, "She doesn't know what she's talking about!" Still, I was happy doing sports with the "A" team. I got there by stepping outside my comfort zone and asking for what I wanted.

By the way, it isn't always crystal clear which path to take. How do you know if you should make the leap? I wish I could give you a guaranteed rule to follow, but there are no guarantees. There are going to be risks. You just have to go back to the heart of who you are and what you want.

At one time a major goal of mine was to be the network TV host of the Olympic Games. The Olympics have always held an allure for me. I'm enthralled by everything about them—the spirit of global competition, the awesome talent of the competitors, the inspiring personal stories, and the sheer thrill of the games. I always held out the hope that one day I'd be in the broadcast booth (and I still do).

When I was working at ESPN in the early 1990s, I received an interesting proposal. I was being considered for a job hosting the syndicated show *American Gladiators*. It was a program featuring muscular athletes competing against everyday athletes. The competitions were bizarre, to say the least. The rules were pretty different from the usual sports competition. Among other things, the gladiators would try to knock each other off high wires and slam each other with heavy objects. Not exactly events we'll be seeing in the Olympics anytime soon!

American Gladiators was an extremely popular show, and they were willing to pay me a ton of money. I could host the show and continue to work at ESPN. In many ways, it was an unbelievable opportunity. But I wondered if hosting *American Gladiators* would hurt my credibility. In particular, I wondered if it would lessen my chances of one day hosting the Olympics. I didn't know, and it was driving me crazy. How could I find out?

My agent at the time, Barry Frank, hit on a solution. "Why don't you call Dick Ebersol at NBC," he suggested. "NBC Sports holds the broadcast rights to the Games. He's the one who hires broadcasters for the Olympics." Wow. Why didn't I think of that?

It took a little nerve. I'd only met Dick once at an awards program. But I picked up the phone and left a message. I didn't really expect him to call me back, but he did—and pretty quickly, too.

I got right to the point: Would hosting *American Gladiators* negatively affect my chances of his hiring me to work on the Olympics one day? He told me he thought I'd already established a lot of credibility at ESPN. Joining *Gladiators* wouldn't necessarily hurt me, but it wasn't a career booster either. Dick knew that *Gladiators* would mean a big payday for me, and he didn't want to stand in the way. I appreciated his professionalism, candor, and warmth, and I think he knew how much I valued his opinion. I passed on *American Gladiators*. I had never taken a job for the money, and I wasn't about to start.

There is a certain mentality in our culture: Always go with the money. I know many people who think that taking a pay cut or turning down a more lucrative job is going backward. I just don't get that mentality. If you're dragging yourself into work every day, how is that anyone's definition of success? Now, I have to be honest. I'm single, and I make good money, so I have it easier than most people. It's expensive raising a family. But I still believe that when you make choices solely based on the money, you're digging a hole. I've met many highly paid, *miserable* people. What good is money if you're not whistling on your way to work?

In 1992, I did get to cover my first Olympics, in Barcelona. The beauty of being at ESPN was that we didn't have to be the broadcast-rights holder. We had an audience who followed us, and they expected coverage of every sports event. If it were the National Tiddly Winks Championship, they would have expected us to cover it. So I went to Barcelona as host for *SportsCenter.*

It was a thrill just to be there, and I was in Barcelona for quite a while. When you're on assignment at the Olympics, you're there for weeks beforehand, setting up and doing background stories. You share an apartment with other members of the crew, and you really get to know one another.

Before the games we worked hard, and sometimes we got a little punchy because we were working crazy hours. The time difference between Spain and Connecticut was big, so we'd be feeding tape at two o'clock in the morning. Then we'd go out to eat. Barcelona is wide-awake at two a.m., and we'd go to the crowded, busy main boulevard, Las Ramblas, and eat fantastic food, then return to work.

Naturally, the close quarters and heavy schedule gave rise to practical jokes, and we played them competitively. On one of our final days before the start of the Games, I came back to the office after dinner with the crew, and the office manager said, "Robin, I know you're going to think I'm kidding, but Bill Cosby called."

I laughed. "You must think I was born today."

"Robin, please, I mean it." She pushed a paper into my hand. "You have to be serious. Here's the number."

"Right." I rolled my eyes. "I'm going to call this number, and Mr. Cosby will be there," I said sarcastically. I knew it was a practical joke. I just didn't know where it was heading. The crew was gathered around, and everyone had good poker faces. OK. I decided to play along.

I dialed the number, and a very cultivated male voice answered, "Cosby residence."

I was impressed. They'd really spent a lot of time on this joke.

"Mr. Cosby, please," I said into the phone.

"Who may I say is calling?" he inquired.

"It's Robin Roberts."

"Oh, yes, Miss Roberts," he said, the chill leaving his voice. "He's expecting your call. One moment, please."

I looked out at the curious faces. *You're good!*" I mouthed to them—and then I heard the voice of Bill Cosby on the other end of the line—and right away I realized it *was* Bill Cosby. "Uh, Mr. Cosby," I said as brightly as I could, "you called?"

He told me that he'd called ESPN because he hadn't seen me on my regular Sunday morning show. He was afraid they'd let me go. They told him I was in Barcelona, and he asked for the number. "I just wanted to make sure everything's cool, and they didn't get rid of you."

"No, sir," I said. I was stunned. I'd been working at ESPN for less than two years, and Bill Cosby was tracking me down in Barcelona to make sure every-thing was cool? Wow!

We became good friends over the years, and I learned that Mr. C. takes a real interest in keeping track of young minorities who are up and coming. He has made it a point to watch their backs—just as he was watching mine.

Since my first day working in Mississippi, I was con-stantly asked if I wanted to do news. And my answer was always an adamant NO! Looking back I realize that my posture was somewhat defensive. I thought people wanted me to do news because they didn't think a woman belonged in sports. It just made me dig my heels in more.

I loved sportscasting. I never tired of traveling to major sporting events. I reported from Wimbledon for six years and ate strawberries and cream every time. I couldn't get there as a pro tennis player but I did as a broadcaster. The feeling was every bit as gratifying. There was always something new and different to keep me interested in being a sportscaster. But then I made a move that would open up that world I had rejected so long. This chapter of my career arrived in the guise of the best sportscasting offer of my life. In the mid-1990s, I was offered the job as host of ABC's *Wide World of Sports*. I had given up my spot on *NFL Primetime* so I could explore opportunities like this. I had watched that show, with its incomparable host, Jim McKay, all my life. It was must-see TV. Who could forget Jim McKay's rich voice and his famous line, "the thrill of victory and the agony of defeat?"

To be a *SportsCenter* anchor AND the host of ABC's *Wide World of Sports* was more than even I could have imagined. Before my first show, Jim McKay himself called the control room to wish me luck. He's such a class act.

Since I was at ABC most weekends hosting *Wide World*, the folks at *Good Morning America Sunday* asked if I could file sports stories for them from time to time. The cohosts were Willow Bay and Bill Ritter, and they made me feel like part of the team. My reports were well received, and before long the executives at *Good Morning America* were also asking me to do sports stories for them. When Willow Bay, who has always been a big supporter of mine, announced that she was leaving *GMA Sunday*, the producer,

Doc Jarden, approached me about filling in for Willow as cohost with Bill Ritter. And just like that I was facing my big moment of truth. Not only did I love sports, but I still had that voice inside of me saying I would be letting women down if I left sportscasting. I wrestled with the decision. Was it time to venture into new territory, to expand my horizons? Doc Jarden, sensing my apprehension, wisely suggested that I would be helping the team if I accepted. I had always been a team player, so I said yes. I also said yes because the time was right. I couldn't have guessed then how much the decision would change my life.

Before long I was doing human-interest stories during the week for *GMA*. And then I was filling in for Diane Sawyer as cohost with Charlie Gibson. The first time I filled in for Diane in 1999, I was so nervous. It was moments before we were going on the air, and my right knee was bobbing up and down under the desk (a family trait—we all do it when we're excited). Charlie reached down, gently placed his hand on my wildly bobbing knee and said, "Darlin', don't worry; you're going to be just fine." And I was.

I had chosen to give myself the benefit of the doubt, to resist becoming stagnant, to see what other possibilities were out there for me. It dawned on me that I was limiting myself by just doing sports. Keep in mind that when I'd started sportscasting, it was all about the game, but in recent years I'd been covering more and more serious news stories around sports—AIDS with Arthur Ashe and Magic Johnson; the O. J. Simpson trial; the Mike Tyson trial; the steroid scandal. The truth was, I'd always said I didn't want to do news, but I was already doing news—and I enjoyed it. But when I was asked to become a full-time *GMA* coanchor in early 2005, it was a big decision. I didn't want to disappoint all the young women who looked up to me as a role model. I was afraid I'd be letting them down. When I mentioned my concern to Billie Jean King, who'd been my role model and had become a friend, she said, "Robin, snap out of it. You'll take all of us with you, and when you do talk about women in sports, you'll have a bigger platform." That's what I love about Billie Jean. She's so open and inclusive. And she was right. The idea of having a broader audience appealed to me—not just sports fans, but all kinds of people with varying interests would be tuning in. Instead of frat boys running up to me chanting the ESPN theme song, *da-da-da, da-da-da*, moms driving minivans were stopping me! For the viewers, *GMA* was like a family, and I was honored to be invited into millions of homes for breakfast every morning. Hope you don't mind that I prefer tea to coffee. One sugar, please. I also realized that as a *GMA* anchor, I was a more visible role model for young women.

There is a difference between running *from* something and running *to* something. For me, *Good Morning America* definitely represented running *to* my future. Not only would I do news; I realized that I *wanted* to do news. Reflecting on the change in my career, I thought about how calculated and well planned my journey in sportscasting had been, yet how serendipitous my landing in news was. I saw that life is both things—plans and surprises. Sometimes you just don't know what you want until you've experienced it.

Being at *GMA* may seem glamorous. I'm sure many people are under the impression that the hosts just work from seven to nine a.m. every day. It may come as a shock but, no, we don't just work two hours a day. We don't just show up, get all made up, do the show, and then say, "Have a great day," and go and eat bon-bons or Krispy Kreme donuts—my personal favorite since I was a kid.

My day starts at four a.m. I'm at our studios in Times Square by five a.m., and head straight for the makeup room. All the way through college I never used makeup, and my hair was always pulled back in a ponytail. My mom told me when I graduated, "Honey, I love you and you are God's child, but natural beauty will take you only so far." It takes almost an hour for my wonderful makeup and hair people—Team Beauty, I call them—to get me TV-ready. I'm squirming in the chair the entire time. Before we go on the air we have a production meeting where we discuss in detail the morning's program.

GMA is challenging and tests all a broadcaster's skills. One moment you're interviewing a world leader or someone who has just been through a tragedy—the next moment you're chatting up the hottest movie star or whipping up something in the kitchen with Emeril Lagasse. I learned a lot by watching two of the best: Charlie Gibson and Diane Sawyer. I cried like a baby when Charlie left *GMA* after an incredible nineteen years. He is one of the most down-to-earth people I have ever met. Just thinking of him right now makes me smile. Diane never ceases to amaze me. I have never known anyone of her stature who works harder than she does. Being on the set with Diane is kind of like being on the court with Michael Jordan. She elevates my game. She demands so much of herself, it makes everyone around her strive to be better. Plus, she has a wicked sense of humor. She's a hoot!

I am usually at the studio until at least ten a.m., then I go to our main offices uptown. By the time I get there the incredible, tireless *GMA* staff is already hard at work on the next day's show. My afternoon is spent making calls or conducting interviews. It's usually five p.m. before I get back home. And the evening is spent poring over pages of research for the topics I will be discussing on the program the next morning. That's a normal day when there isn't breaking news. It's a hectic schedule. And I relish every second of it. But you don't just fall into having a career like this. I don't know a single successful person who doesn't work harder and smarter than everybody else.

The job calls for a lot of traveling around the world. I was in Kuwait when the Iraq War began in March of 2003. I remember visiting one of the military camps on the border of Iraq. I was struck with how young those brave soldiers were. The day I visited, it was Selection Sunday—also known as "March Madness"—back in the United States. That's the day when all the teams are announced that will be taking part in the NCAA Basketball Tournament. When the young soldiers spotted me, they recognized me from my ESPN days when I covered the tournament. They ran up to me and started asking me question after question. Who were the top seeds in the tourney? Who did I think would win the national championship? How much fun is it to work with the irrepressible Dick Vitale? Here they were, about to go to war, but at that moment all they cared about was whether their favorite team was headed for the Big Dance. I immediately called the assignment desk at ESPN and passed along the precious information to the troops.

Every person is capable of growing and changing. Never forget that. Whether you're twenty or fifty, there's always an opportunity to shift course and reinvent yourself from within. I'm not talking about physically changing direction. I'm talking about the interior changes that make you stronger, kinder, and more connected to the world around you.

In 2006, I was at the U.S. Open when Andre Agassi took his final bow after twenty-one years in the game. I had covered Andre at Wimbledon in the early nineties. I remembered him as the brash Vegas kid with the long hair, the pirate's bandana, and the cocky attitude. He used to say, "Image is everything," and he seemed to live that way. Sure, he was extremely talented, but it all seemed to be superficial. No depth whatsoever. Boy, was I wrong!

Fast-forward to 2006. When he retired from tennis at age thirty-six, Andre was a man, not a boy. He had matured into a husband and father, a responsible adult, an unbelievable role model. He'd personally given away $60 million through the Andre Agassi Charitable Foundation, which helps inner-city kids from Las Vegas get a start in life. He lost his last match, but the fans didn't care. They were on their feet, cheering and screaming for him. When he took the microphone from the courtside reporter, Mary Jo Fernandez, to say a few words to the fans, he was weeping—and so were the rest of us. He was so humble, so full of gratitude. Through his tears he said, "The scoreboard said I lost today, but what the scoreboard doesn't say is what it is I have found. And over the last twenty-one years, I have found loyalty. You have pulled for me on court and also in life. I've found inspiration. You have willed me to succeed sometimes even in my lowest moments. And I've found generosity. You have given me your shoulders to stand on to reach for my dreams, dreams I could never have reached without you. Over the last twenty-one years, I have found you, and I will take you and the memory of you with me for the rest of my life. Thank you."

He had won. It was one of the most beautiful moments I've seen in sports. And it was made even more poignant by the knowledge of the transformation Andre had achieved during his career. Somewhere along the way he made a choice to step up to the plate and live a life of meaning and substance. What an inspiration for all of us. Further proof it's never too late to change our way of thinking.

When I'm talking to groups, young or old, I like to challenge them with this question: "What would you do if you knew you couldn't fail?" I immediately see the faces in the room light up as people imagine the possibilities. Then I tell them, "Go with that feeling. Because it's fear of failure, more than anything else, that will prevent you from having the life you want."

What would it be like if the idea of failing didn't exist? What would it be like if people didn't walk around feeling as if their entire identities were called into question with every misstep? I'll bet you'd see more people spreading their wings and taking flight, with the freedom to be themselves.

Fear is what keeps people in the comfort zone— but here's the rub: There is no comfort zone. Life comes at us in ways we can't predict or control. You get downsized from your job after thirty years and are left with no pension. A hurricane blows your house away. You're diagnosed with a serious illness. As my sister Sally-Ann likes to say, "Life is *live*. You can't rewind it." After 9/11, I was struck by how many people talked about the importance of living each day fully, as they thought about all those people who went to work that fateful morning not knowing it would be for the last time.

So if you really want something, but find yourself hesitating to make a change or pursue an uncertain course, take some time to question yourself: Are your in-laws stopping you? Think it through. What's the worst thing that could happen?

It might not be possible to make a change right now. Maybe there are bills to pay and kids to raise. But you can start planning for the time when it *will* be possible. While you're doing that, look around you and take note of how others do it. Collect their stories. Success leaves clues.

You have to balance pursuing your dream with being practical and realistic. Dream big but focus small. I come across many people who want to make career changes, but they don't have the foggiest idea where to start. This requires creativity. Chances are, if you make a career change you'll have to start at the bottom, and that's harder than you think. It's not just your own willingness to take an entry-level position. You'll find that employers are skeptical of hiring seasoned workers for entry-level positions. Can someone who has spent twenty years managing an office or teaching school adapt to being at the bottom rung?

Not everyone can. You have to convince them that your passion is great enough to put up with a few jolts to your ego.

Last year I met a woman in Chicago who is an educator. She was well respected in her field and had done significant work in her community. Now she wanted to translate that background into a broadcasting job. Occasionally, people get lucky and smoothly make that segue. Look at Rachael Ray. That's not typical, though. I would have recommended to this educator that she start in a smaller market, but moving away from Chicago was not an option; she was older and had a family and children. Chicago is one of the top TV markets in the country. You normally have to have quite a few years of experience in television before you work in the Windy City.

If she hoped to get a foot in the door, this woman had to be creative and persistent. I told her to use her strength—education—because that's what she knows best. I suggested that the next time there were important issues in the city involving education, she should have someone tape her talking about them on a video camera. Then she should contact the TV stations in town and set up meetings with the news directors. Because she is well known in her field, that wouldn't be too hard to arrange. TV stations are often looking for local experts on various topics such as education. I also suggested that she expand her horizons to include radio. And by all means, she should find a network. Take a class, join a group, get involved with people who share her interest. Most people begin their professions right out of college, when they have a built-in network of support, through teachers, other students, internships, and the like. When you're starting fresh later in life, the isolation of your quest can be daunting.

Stepping outside your comfort zone takes an open attitude and a tremendous passion. You have to know before you start how much you're willing to sacrifice, how much time you're willing to dedicate to training and study, and how flexible you are about your work environment. Write down your goals, then list the steps you have to take to get there. What are your strengths? What barriers do you have to overcome? What will success look like?

I am always inspired by the fearless, dedicated people I meet who take on new challenges later in life. My parents were my primary models. My brother, Butch, is a more recent example. Butch has lived in Houston for many years, raising a family and doing well in his career as a stockbroker. A few years ago, when he was in his early fifties, Butch's company was downsizing. He didn't panic for a second. For Butch, the downsizing offered an opportunity to do something he had always wanted to do—teach school. He had a degree in English from Rutgers, but had never used it. He decided that now was the time. Today, Butch is a schoolteacher in Houston, at a time when male role models are desperately needed. His classes include a lot of kids who were relocated after Katrina, making the timing of his career change even more significant.

Butch never really loved being a stockbroker, but he loves being a teacher. I often think of the kids whose lives will be changed because my brother dared to take this step late in life.

By the way, speaking of being outside one's comfort zone, in November 2003, I had a rare chance to experience what it was like to be in my father's shoes as a pilot with the Tuskegee Airmen. Remember my brief flirtation with flying when I was in college? It never went anywhere, which is just as well. I'm not sure I have the nerves of steel required for the job. But when *Good Morning America* did a "fantasy" segment, I swallowed my jitters and said I wanted to fly an aircraft similar to the one my father had flown.

My training (if you can call eight hours training) took place at Moton Field air base in Alabama. Moton Field is where the Tuskegee Airmen trained for their heroic run during World War II. It was hard not to feel the spirits of those brave men who saved thousands of lives during the war.

My parents joined me in Tuskegee. The first day we shot some background scenes and interviews—including one with Dad. The second day I was scheduled to do the flight live on *GMA*. I don't think I'd ever seen my dad so animated. He was normally a pretty reserved guy, but he was really into it. After dinner, as I was giving my parents instructions for the next morning, he asked—as only a parent with two kids in television would—"Do I need to wear the same outfit for *continuity?*" I thought that was so cute. I assured him he could wear whatever he wanted. "Good," he said. "I want to wear my red blazer, because that's what the Airmen wore."

The next morning there was a small crowd of us

on the airfield. My sister Dorothy had brought her two daughters, Jessica and Lauren, because she wanted them to experience this piece of history. Dad was standing tall in his red blazer, beaming. Mom was smiling too, although she looked a little nervous.

When I'd interviewed Dad the previous day, I asked him how he felt being an Airman at a time when African Americans didn't have a lot of rights in this country. He reminded me that the black unit was considered an experiment—in fact, it was called the Tuskegee Experiment, which is a distasteful characterization, to say the least. But there was nothing experimental about it, as far as Dad and the other Airmen were concerned. "We knew we couldn't fail," he said. "We *wouldn't* fail."

I asked him what it was like to fly, and he told me something I had never heard him say before. He said, "Flying was the only time I felt completely free. It's what I loved about flying." It touched me deeply when he said that. I was glad I could spotlight the Tuskegee Airmen and bring the story of their bravery and achievements into so many homes through *GMA*. It was another one of those "Aha!" moments, when I thought, *I know why I'm meant to do this*. I treasure the memory of that day, because less than a year later, my father passed away.

I had said I wanted to fly a plane like my dad's. I didn't mean I wanted to fly the *same* plane. When that sucker came chugging down the runway, I wondered what I had got myself into. It was old school—an authentic A-T6. My dad was going, "Yeah!" I was going, "Uh-oh."

Taking off on my televised flight was magical, a dream come true. I wanted to pinch myself, thinking, *I'm flying!* It was one more confirmation for me that anything is possible if you're open to it. In fact, it was such a wonderful experience that I decided I really did want to get my license and become a pilot, after all. I haven't done it yet. Hey, I've got to have something out there to strive for. Keeps life interesting.

After the segment, I was flooded with letters. People would share their stories with me. They loved the bond they saw between my father and me, and they told me how they'd been "Daddy's girl" too. It was such a personal connection.

I want to add that in March 2006 the Tuskegee Airmen were awarded the Congressional Gold Medal. It's the highest and most distinguished award in the nation. (The first recipient was George Washington!) I wish my father had lived to see that. He would have been proud. But I know he would have also said that they never did it for the glory. They did it because it was their job, and because it was the right thing to do.

6. Focus on the Solution, Not the Problem

Less than twelve hours after Hurricane Katrina made landfall on Monday, August 29, 2005, I left my home in New York City and jumped on a plane with the *Good Morning America* crew headed for the Gulf Coast. As a journalist, it was second nature for me to rush into the center of disaster to report events as they happen. But Katrina was more than a professional assignment. This, my friends, was personal.

The Mississippi Coast is my home. Although I'd lived up north for more than fifteen years working for ABC and ESPN, Pass Christian will always be home.

My family still has a house in the Pass, which my siblings and I call "our house," even after our parents moved to a second home in Biloxi to be closer to the medical services at Keesler Air Force Base. We still celebrated Christmas every year at the Pass house.

The last time I had spoken with my mother on Sunday, the day before Katrina hit, she was hunkered down in her Biloxi house with my sister Dorothy and her two girls, Jessica, age twenty, and Lauren, seventeen. They had decided to stay. Mom's health issues made it difficult for her to evacuate, and my sister and nieces left their own home in nearby Long Beach to be with her. If you're lucky you have a sibling who lives close to your folks. It's especially comforting when you have aging parents. That's our Dorothy. My family tried not to be too worried. They had weathered some ferocious storms in their day, starting with Hurricane Camille in 1969, when I was eight years old. As Katrina came ashore, Mom's final words to me before I lost contact with her were, "We're not to be fearful. Wherever we are, God is." It was this strong faith that had sustained Mom after my father's death the previous fall, and for all of her eighty-two years.

I'm not going to lie. I wished I had talked my mother and sister into taking shelter inland. As I headed for the Gulf Coast, I grew increasingly anxious. I had been unable to get a call through since Katrina hit. Driving through the darkness after our plane landed in Lafayette, Louisiana, two hundred miles from Biloxi, all I could do was hope and pray. As my crew tried to work out the details of how we'd be able to broadcast the next morning, my head was filled with the plea, *Please, God, let me find my mom, my sister, my family . . . let them be OK.*

I could hardly get my head around the fact that just a week earlier my family had been together for a joyful occasion. Sally-Ann's oldest daughter, Judith, was starting medical school at Howard University—my parents' alma mater. We'd all traveled to Washington, D.C., to attend Judith's white-coat ceremony. This is a beautiful ritual where the new medical students receive their white coats and are welcomed into a noble profession with a charge to do good. I thought Mom would burst with pride. She and Dad had always wanted us kids to attend Howard University, and none of us had. But here was Judith, fulfilling their dream. It was such a happy, hopeful day.

None of us could have anticipated that a week later we'd be hit by an enormous disaster. That's the way of life. You can't always be physically prepared, but as I made my way toward the Pass, I was praying that I'd have the spiritual resources to confront whatever awaited me there.

It was a rough ride. We steered through an obstacle course of downed power lines, abandoned cars, and the rubble of houses and stores torn to pieces. An overturned tanker in the distance looked like a toy on the road. It took all night to cover those two hundred miles.

At five a.m. Tuesday morning we reached Pass Road and began to slowly make our way toward the heart of Biloxi. That's when the magnitude of the devastation hit me. I have traveled Pass Road for almost four decades, and I know it like the back of my hand. But I was completely lost. Where were all the familiar landmarks, all the comfortable signs of home? One of my producers, Brian O'Keefe, kept asking me how far it was to my mother's house. I didn't know!

In the end I needed a police escort to find Mom's house. I will never forget the compassion of Officer Ryan Frazier. When we finally reached the house, I could see damage to the roof, but otherwise it didn't look too bad. I ran up to the door, Officer Frazier following with a huge flashlight. I simply don't have the words to describe my emotions as I walked in and saw my mom safe and sound. It felt so good to hug her close. She whispered in my ear, "I knew you would find me."

When my sister Dorothy saw the bright light from Officer Frazier's flashlight she screamed, "No TV! No TV camera!" As if I could be thinking about work at a time like this. But, you know, Dorothy was not entirely wrong. In this moment, my personal and professional lives did intersect. It was only because of my job that I was able to get home and see my loved ones, while countless others were still praying for some word. And once I made sure my family was OK, I rushed back to the satellite truck, trying not to think of my family's close call.

Later, Mom described for me how the wind howled and shook the house, carrying off a portion of the roof and slamming a tree against one side. "The screams of the wind were so loud, I thought we were going to take off into flight," she said. She regretted not evacuating. She told me that during the worst of the storm, a verse from an old Bible song she learned as a child in Akron kept replaying in her head. It was about Jonah and the whale: *"He'll just make you willing to go . . . He will not compel you to go against your will . . . He'll just make you willing to go."* She smiled, remembering. "I said, 'Lord, next time I'll be willing to go. This will be the last time I sit through a storm.'" I knew she meant it, and I'm going to hold her to it.

Good Morning America went live at 6:00 a.m. local time from Pass Road, not far from my mother's house. I reported on the incredible destruction I had seen, trying to convey to people across the nation what it was like for folks down on the Gulf Coast. I was doing OK, maintaining my journalistic objectivity, holding my feelings in check. I had a job to do, and I needed to put my personal situation aside. But then my coanchor Charlie Gibson started asking me if my family was all right. "Your mom's OK? Your sisters are OK?" He kept at me. All at once, the feelings caught up with me—the emotional tide that had been building for the past twenty-fours hours. I broke down and cried on the air. At first I thought, *Oh, no, I'm going to lose my job.* You're not supposed to show emotion on TV like that. Plus, I'm not one to let things get to me. Being an athlete taught me that. So did the strength and determination of my parents. But there I was, weeping.

Only one other time in my life had I experienced grief coming over me in this way, and that was when my father died. I was in the composure business. You have to be when you're on TV. Work now, cry later. But my tears had a life of their own. They were going to flow whether I wanted them to or not. And by now I realized it was OK.

The next day, I was weeping again. The police finally let me into Pass Christian, and I made a beeline for our house. I was relieved to find it still standing. I couldn't go inside because the locks were corroded from saltwater, but I peeked in through a broken window and saw where the water line had been, high on the wall near the ceiling. I was thankful that the damage had not been worse.

I headed downtown. It was surreal. The park with the tennis courts where I had spent my youth dreaming of playing at Wimbledon was gone. My high school, once a picturesque redbrick building, was reduced to rubble. Seeing my town, the center of my childhood, wiped out, was overwhelming. The tears came again. I could have handled seeing our house flattened, because you can rebuild a house. But how do you rebuild an entire town?

I'm rarely at a loss for words, but the devastation and the raw need left me speechless. People were desperate for the most basic things. Our satellite truck had a phone, and people were lining up like they were at a phone booth, anxious to connect with loved ones outside the area. We'd brought cases of water, energy bars, and nonperishables, and the supply was quickly gone. Faced with such need, we gave what we could—but it was so inadequate.

Sally-Ann had sent her twelve-year-old son Jeremiah to Atlanta with a group from her church, and her daughter Kelly was also out of the area with friends. Sally-Ann stayed behind to broadcast for WWL-TV from a makeshift studio located in Baton Rouge. She had seen my report from the Coast and that's how she first learned that Mom, Dorothy, and the girls were OK.

I was also concerned about my friends Cheryl and Luella. I wanted to know that they and their families were safe. Both of them were happily married to their high-school sweethearts, and they'd remained in the area. I was especially worried about Cheryl, who lived in what had been her grandmother's house, on Hiern Avenue, right in the center of the storm. There were no working phones, so I decided to walk over there, but I couldn't even find Hiern Avenue. I left word around town that I was looking for Cheryl and Luella, praying that my friends were OK. When they showed up at the satellite truck, we just hugged one another. Words couldn't describe what we were feeling. Cheryl and Luella visited several times while we were broadcasting. When the crew saw them coming, they'd call out, "The True Blues are here!" It was so comforting for me. But I could see how stunned they were by the damage. I was painfully aware that I would soon be flying back to my comfortable, intact existence, while my friends and family faced an uncertain future.

The day our *GMA* crew was scheduled to leave, I begged my mother to come back with me. Everything was too tenuous down there. I wanted to know she was safe. She told me she'd come with me if the plane was big enough to fit the whole Mississippi Gulf Coast. Otherwise, she was staying. That was my mother—but this time I was upset by her serenity and determination. We argued back and forth, and

I'll bet you can guess who won. Finally, Mom shoved me out the door. "Be our voice of the Gulf Coast," she instructed.

As I sat on the plane waiting for our gear to be loaded, I was filled with anxiety. I kept thinking that I shouldn't be leaving. I should stay and help my mom and sister put their lives back together. Dorothy's home in Long Beach, Mississippi, was severely damaged. I should stay and help Sally-Ann, whose house in New Orleans was underwater. She'd had to face the chaos without her beloved husband, Willie, who had died of cancer in November 2002. The whole family was affected in some way. Butch's wife Cynthia's family lived in New Orleans, and their homes were destroyed. They moved in with Butch and Cynthia in Houston. At one point there were twelve additional people crowded into the house.

Everyone was pitching in to help family. I felt the pull of family stronger than anything else. I turned to my producer, Sarah Ruth. "What am I doing?" I said. "I can't leave. I can't leave my family." I started to get up from my seat. "I'm getting off this plane."

Sarah reached out a hand. "Robin," she said, "you can do more good for your family from the outside. Think about how many people watch our show every morning. You can get the word out."

I sank back into my seat. She was right. I thought of all the people who had said to me, over and over, "Please don't forget us. Please don't forget us." I had lost my bearings for a moment. I needed to focus on the solution, not the problem—but how?

I returned to New York, but I was numb. My mind and heart were back in Mississippi. Then *GMA* came up with an idea. Our then executive producer, Ben Sherwood, said, "We're going to adopt your home town."

"Huh?" I didn't understand. We didn't do that sort of thing in the news business—at least, that's what I thought.

He explained that the outpouring from viewers had been so great after they saw me crying on air, that ABC had decided they must respond. "We are being inundated with calls and letters and e-mails from people all over the country wanting to help, wondering what they can do," he said. "Let's bring our viewers together with the people who need their help." I was suddenly reinvigorated and confident that this was where I belonged.

A few weeks later, I was blessed to return to the Pass and announce that GMA was making a yearlong commitment to help my hometown get back on its feet. We would document the recovery effort on the program. We'd also be on the ground lending a hand and linking our viewers with our partners in rebuilding—the Salvation Army and the Corporation for National and Community Service. I felt so grateful that I could be used to bring together those in need with those who wanted to help. Then, the following April, our parent company, Disney, donated $1.5 million to help restore sixteen boys and girls clubs on the Gulf Coast—including the one in Pass Christian that had been cofounded by my parents.

While I was home, Dorothy and I brought Mom to the Pass Christian house for the first time. We all had tears in our eyes, looking at our home of thirty years, the first floor completely ruined and cherished mementos washed away. But Mom was her usual practical, optimistic self. "All is not lost," she announced. "It will just take time to rebuild."

There is nothing more empowering than focusing on the solution instead of the problem. You draw strength from your own ability to get through it, to conquer the hopelessness. I was astounded by the response generated by *GMA*'s call for help. It was awesome. For example, I had said on the air that there was a great need for chainsaws, and I encountered a man from Tennessee who had set up a place in town where you could get chainsaws. "I saw you on the air," he said. "So I came down." When I asked him how long he planned to stay, he shrugged. "Well, as long as we're needed."

That's just one of many, many stories. People wanted to help. I firmly believe that it is inherent to human nature to want to lift others up. We were all in it together.

Being a journalist has exposed me to tragedy and suffering all over the world. I have seen despair, but I have also seen that no matter how great the problem, there are always people dedicated to the solution. In the summer of 2005, I traveled to South Africa with former President Bill Clinton, to check on his foundation's projects in the battle against AIDS. Clinton's work is an inspiring example of practical action. His foundation focuses on getting antiretroviral medicine (called ARVs)—and they go straight to the source, the pharmaceutical companies. Over and over, the former president made the point that we have the tools to beat this, we have the medications to extend life. We need to get the medication to the people who need it.

We traveled to Lesotho, a tiny African kingdom, where one in three people is infected with the AIDS virus. Can you imagine that? The average life expectancy is thirty-seven years old. And so many of the victims are children. It just breaks your heart. I was constantly moved by the warm, personal connection Clinton had with the children. Their faces just lit up in his presence. He told me, "You look at these children, and you see that they are the same as children everywhere. They should have the same life."

While we visited one ravaged community after another, I certainly expected to shed some tears. What came as a complete surprise to me was that there would be so many tears of joy. One day I came upon a group of women dancing. I asked them afterward, through a translator, "Why are you dancing?" They replied, "We're celebrating life." Imagine such an indomitable spirit.

I also had the opportunity to interview Rita Marley, wife of the late, great Bob Marley. For twenty years Rita has been working to eradicate poverty in Africa and Jamaica through the Bob Marley Foundation and the Rita Marley Foundation. In life Bob Marley was deeply committed to empowering others, and Rita has dedicated her life to carrying on his work, in the most tangible ways possible. Her absolute commitment is an inspiration. "It's important that you can be an example to someone, somewhere, and somehow," she said simply.

I know that some people may be thinking, Well, it's easy for President Clinton or Rita Marley to make a difference. They have resources and connections. But the key to solving problems is the underlying desire to do it. I've seen people make miracles happen just because they decided they were going to focus on the solution, not the problem. I think of my interview with Benita Singh and Ruth DeGolia, recent graduates from Yale University, who did just that. While they were at Yale, the young women spent nine months in Guatemala's western highlands, where they were amazed by the beautiful jewelry and handicrafts made by the local women.

They knew people back home would fall in love with these items, if only they had a way to take them there. On the spot, they decided to launch an initiative that would link six women's cooperatives to the U.S. market. They bought two suitcases full of items, and went back to campus, where they sold them at a 300 percent profit. Fast-forward, they now have a company called Mercado Global that provides the marketing for these Guatemalan women. The first year there was a profit of $75,000 for the company; the second year it was $600,000, with 90 percent of the money going right back to the women in the cooperative.

Benita and Ruth were kids. They had no special resources. There was no blueprint. They simply saw a need, and they decided to help these women help themselves. They demonstrated that if you're open and receptive, and you're willing to act, you can find a way to turn a problem into a solution.

In August 2006, I returned to the Gulf Coast for the one-year anniversary of Hurricane Katrina. Before my trip home I interviewed former President Bill

Clinton. He and the first President Bush had raised more than $130 million the past year for hurricane relief. President Clinton told me it was important that people on the Coast and in New Orleans shouldn't be made to feel they are a "problem to be managed." He spoke with genuine feeling when he said, "They are an asset for tomorrow."

When I landed at the airport in Gulfport, Mississippi, a few days before the anniversary, a woman came up to me in baggage claim. Her name was Barbara and she was from Pass Christian. She began to thank me for *GMA*'s assistance in the Pass, then she burst into tears. She and her family had lost their home and were now living in Philadelphia. She, too, had come back for the anniversary. We comforted each other and shared wonderful stories of the Pass. It had been a year, but the pain of all that had been lost was still very much on the surface for many.

I spent time with First Lady Laura Bush at an elementary school in Biloxi. Her foundation has raised more than one million dollars to restore school libraries in Mississippi and Louisiana. When I asked Mrs. Bush, a former librarian, about the importance of devoting money to school libraries she said, "The point is to get schools up and running again. People want to come back home. But they can't come home if there aren't schools open for their children."

I appreciated her making that point. I'd noticed that many people who had been eager to help in the beginning were getting "passion fatigue" after a year. As a nation we have attention deficit disorder when it comes to disasters. People say, "Why aren't you over it? Why haven't you rebuilt?" But it's a long process. And from a practical standpoint, the people of the Gulf Coast can't rebuild until they know what the infrastructure is going to be—whether there will be schools and libraries and banks and grocery stores nearby. In New Orleans, my sister Sally-Ann is waiting to find out if they're going to rebuild the school her son Jeremiah goes to. These are complicated practical matters, and they have to be faced in the midst of enormous loss.

When I spoke with President Clinton, he said that it usually takes three years after a disaster until you can start judging the comeback. The first year is shock and grieving and picking up the pieces. Putting those pieces back together is a longer task.

Two hundred and thirty-one people died in Mississippi because of Katrina, including Sam and Matthew Tart of Pass Christian. Geno Tart was working the overnight shift in a mental-health center as Katrina approached. Her husband, Sam, and two-year-old son, Matthew, remained at home. Sam had been through Hurricane Camille, and he thought everything would be OK. When Geno returned home the next morning, neighbors can still remember her screams. Her family had drowned in their home. It was Matthew's second birthday. You wonder how any human being could possibly recover from the horror of that day. A year later we talked to Geno, and I'll never forget her words. This woman who had lost everything said, "For those who have survived, keep your faith and everything will be just fine." Then she smiled sweetly. What unshakeable courage and strength.

The morning of the anniversary we broadcasted live from War Memorial Park in Pass Christian. The legendary Patti LaBelle was there, along with the Grammy-winning gospel duo Mary Mary, who joined a local church choir to lift our spirits with song. It was the sound of hope. Before the storm, my hometown had about 6,500 residents. A year later, less than half remained, and I think just about all of them were in

War Memorial Park with us that morning. We reflected on the year and thanked the more than 8,000 volunteers who had come to the Pass to help.

We mourned all that we lost but also celebrated what we had gained. My mom, who was with me that morning, perhaps said it best, "It's been a time of reawakening to not only what we had that's gone, but what we can rebuild and do."

I was struck by how frequently in life we are tested by adversity. If we allow ourselves to use it as a lesson and a path forward, we can emerge from our pain on the other side, stronger and more alive than before. One of my favorite stories tells of a butterfly's cocoon. Someone sees the movement of the butterfly pressing against the wall of the cocoon, and they think they'll help it along and just cut a little hole in the cocoon so the butterfly can come on out with ease. But the butterfly dies soon after. There's a reason why it's beating its wings against the wall of the cocoon—to make it stronger. That's the way I like to think about the trials we go through. They're meant to make us stronger.

One more story about the spirit of the Gulf Coast— and wouldn't you know it's about sports. On September 25, 2006, the New Orleans Superdome—the center of so much suffering and despair during Hurricane Katrina—opened its doors for the return of the city's beloved Saints. It had taken $180 million and an incredible physical effort to restore the stadium in just a little more than a year's time. But now the Saints would come marching in to play their archrival, the Atlanta Falcons. The whole city was delirious with anticipation.

I was lucky to be in town as part of the pregame show with Chris Berman and Bob Ley, wearing my ESPN hat. The morning of the game I had breakfast with Sally-Ann. She's not a big sports fan, but that day she was wearing black and gold for the Saints. We talked about how some people had criticized the city for making the restoration of the Superdome a priority, when so many people are unable to move back into their neighborhoods. Sally-Ann was still living in someone else's house, and her son Jeremiah was sleeping in a closet, but she thought it was important to get the Superdome up and running. She told me that the whole city was obsessed with the Saints–Falcons game. "When your life has been torn apart and you don't know if it's ever going to be the same again, you just crave a semblance of normalcy," she said. "Today we have this moment when we can root for the Saints, and it's so wonderful to see the smiles on everyone's faces. We're Saints fans again, not victims."

That night inside the Superdome, the mood was electric. It's the only way I know how to describe it. I looked out from my booth into the sea of 70,000 faces—smiling, laughing, crying—and I just realized again what these people had gone through. Just to see the happiness—it was unforgettable.

During most of the pregame show, we'd been broadcasting for the folks at home, while we watched the Superdome fill up with fans. When it came time to introduce the two bands, U2 and Green Day, we opened our mikes to the house. I started to say, "We're bringing the music back to New Orleans . . ." and 70,000 people started screaming and hollering and clapping and pounding their feet. It was a huge roar. Chris Berman said, "Your picture is on the JumboTron." They were screaming for me, the hometown girl. And I think they were voicing their appreciation for the work we'd done over the past year. I just sat there, filled with an intense sense of belonging.

After the bands played, I closed the pregame show by speaking to them from the heart, and they responded once again—especially at the end when I shouted, "Let's go to the game!"

I wanted so badly to stay and watch the game—to just be a fan. But I had to get back to New York for the morning show, so I left the stadium as the teams were taking the field. The Superdome was rocking, and I thought to myself, *This is the power of sports.* What else could we have done that would have made people feel this way? I couldn't think of anything.

I know that God doesn't take sides in sporting events, no matter how much we pray for victory. But He must have made an exception this one time. The Saints crushed the Falcons, 23–3.

7. Keep Faith, Family, and Friends Close to Your Heart

Most parents stress the importance of the three "R's"—reading, 'riting, and 'rithmatic. My folks taught us the three "D's"—discipline, determination, and Da Lord. Going to church was mandatory. If you were too sick to go to church, you were too sick to go out and play for the rest of the weekend. Later, when I was a young adult and making my own choices, I found myself still in church. Spirituality comforts me. It's a bond I share with my family.

When I'm on the phone with Sally-Ann, she always has to end with a prayer. I'll be on my cell, walking down the street, and I'll say, "I'm going into a bagel shop," and she'll say, "No, no, just wait. We have to pray." So I'll stop and listen to Sally-Ann pray, then I'll say, "Amen!" and get some funny looks from people passing me. My colleagues at the office are used to it, though. If they pass my office and see me on the phone with my eyes closed, they'll say, "She's talking to Sally-Ann."

My Grandma Sally always read a daily devotional called *Streams in the Desert*. Each devotional begins with a passage from the Bible, followed by a lesson. My mother gave my siblings and me our own copies when each of us was in high school. I cannot express how powerful it is to know that my entire family is reading the same passage as I am every morning.

After Grandma Sally died, I received her copy of *Streams in the Desert*, with her handwritten notes in the margins. I love having her copy. I treasure seeing her handwriting. It's so calming to read her simple little reflections, tucked in the corners of the pages. They are just as powerful as the words in the book. The first time I read her note, "Help me not to leave anything undone that I can do, Lord," I got tears in my eyes.

My siblings and I have all achieved success in our respective careers. But my mom always says the greatest thrill we give her is when someone tells her, "I saw your child in church."

When I first moved away from Mississippi to work in Nashville, my mom gave me another gift of prayer—what she called the 2 L's and 2 P's of God. As the early morning sports anchor for WSMV, I would be leaving my apartment at 4:30 a.m. (What is it about me and early morning TV shows?) It would still be dark outside, and I would be a single woman living alone in a strange city. My mother told me to say the Prayer of Protection before I opened my door and walked outside, and no harm would come to me. It goes:

The Light of God surrounds me,
The Love of God enfolds me,
The Power of God protects me,
The Presence of God watches over me,
Wherever I am, God is.

I have said that prayer every morning over the past twenty years. Several years ago I shared it with viewers of *Good Morning America*. Barely a week has gone by since that I haven't received a request for the prayer.

I once asked my mother why she thought her four children had been so successful in life, while others in the family were less so. She replied without hesitation: "Manners."

"What?" I wasn't really expecting that.

"You kids were taught manners. You were taught how to do things. How to act. Many people don't teach their kids how to be civil anymore."

I had to laugh a little, remembering how it was for us. Perhaps it stemmed partly from my dad's military background. We were expected to behave at the dinner table—no elbows on the table, one hand in our laps. When I was out with my friends they'd look at me like I was a big nerd, but it was easier to endure their teasing than to challenge my parents on this central point.

Manners aren't just about saying "Please pass the salt." They're fundamentally about respect—for others and for yourself. I'm glad my parents stressed manners, because I learned a fundamental attitude of respect. Unfortunately, this lesson has gone unlearned by many kids today, even when their parents emphasize it. One of my nieces was visiting me in New York last summer, and we were having dinner. Her cell phone rang, and she picked it up, listened, and said, "Hold on." Then she hung up the phone.

First of all, I wasn't pleased with her for answering the phone during dinner. But I was curious. "What was that about?" I asked.

She explained, "I gave my number to a guy last night, and I thought I'd given him the wrong number, but I guess I gave him the right number."

I was flabbergasted. "So, you just hung up on him? You said 'hold on,' and then you hung up on him?' "

She shrugged. "That's how we do it." I could see she thought her old fogy aunt didn't understand. I understood, all right. I just didn't like it. "You call him back," I said. "Tell him you're sorry. Tell him anything. But don't just disrespect him. It took guts for him to call you." I gave her my sternest look. "And what are you doing giving him your number, anyway?"

She seemed a bit deflated. "Yes, ma'am," she said, and went off to make the call. I wished I didn't sound so much like my mother, but it was important. I grew up believing that bad manners create bad karma. It doesn't take that much effort to be respectful.

My mother also stressed the importance of using proper grammar, not ebonics or Southern slang. If I asked, "Where's Daddy at?" she would reply, "Between the *a* and the *t*." You didn't end a sentence with a preposition in our house. If I said I was done with my chores, Mom would respond, "I didn't know you were cooking." I was *finished* with my chores.

I remember when I was in the third grade, a little boy called me a name. I went home and asked my mother, "Mom, what's a *blackbitch*?" I said it like it was one word. My mother didn't get all upset about the slur. She simply replied, with careful schoolteacher diction, "First of all, it's two words: black bitch." I still chuckle when I think of it.

As I got older, when I left my mother a note explaining where I was, that note would be corrected in red ink and left waiting for me when I returned. We didn't have spell check when we were growing up. We had my mother. If we asked her how to spell a word, she always made us sound it out and try to figure out how to spell it ourselves. As a child, I hated the constant corrections. As an adult, I came to realize what an important point she was making. As a journalist, I thank her every day.

Even now, Mom doesn't hesitate to tell me when she thinks I'm getting lazy with my pronunciation. She'll call me up after a show and say, "It's CHAM-PI-ON-SHIP, not *champ'ynship*." People can always tell when I've been home to Mississippi. My enunciation is so clear that the word S-M-I-L-E sounds like it has five syllables.

My mother was also insistent about our reading. We weren't allowed to "veg out" in front of the TV. She often said, "Reading opens up the mind and imagination." She had book clubs for Butch and Sally-Ann, because they were such avid readers. They still are.

My parents were the first in their families to go to college. It means a lot to them that all four of their children earned college degrees. I think it has also meant a lot to them that we have all found ways of making a contribution in the world. They were pleased when Butch decided to teach school in Houston, and I know they have always been incredibly proud of the good work my sisters do. Dorothy, who is four years older than I am and my closest sibling in age, is a dedicated and caring social worker. She has chosen to focus on the lost youth in Mississippi—those troubled adolescents whose brushes with the law have brought them to the attention of the Mississippi Department of Mental Health. As the social service director at the Specialized Treatment Facility, Dorothy develops programs designed to heal their hearts and minds. It's tough work. We always say that she's the one in the family who is absolutely guaranteed a place in heaven. She'll leave our names at the gate. I can imagine her there, singing, as she has one of the most beautiful voices I've ever heard.

Sally-Ann has been my inspiration in many ways, and she is an inspiration to her community, too. She believes so much in the importance of mentors that she started the "Each One, Save One" program, which has partnered hundreds of local students with volunteers in the business community for one-on-one mentoring.

I get a lot more notoriety than my siblings, but they are all every bit as successful—if not more so. In many ways I've had it easier. Being a single woman, I haven't had to juggle the demands of a family with the work I love. My three siblings have eight children among them, and although I have no kids of my own, I get as much "Auntie time" as possible. I'm challenged by them and proud of them. Butch and Cynthia have three children and are experiencing the joys of being grandparents. Their daughter Bianca has two children, Jazzlyn and Braylon; and their daughter Renée has a daughter, Ashley. Their son, Lawrence III, was a second-round draft pick in the 2005 NBA Draft. I can't tell you how exhilarating it is to have a nephew playing pro ball.

Lawrence has a lot of character, and he needs it in order to negotiate the tough world of sports—whether it's college or pro. When he was a junior at Mississippi State, he could have gone to the NBA, but he chose to return to school for his senior year. I admired him for making that choice. Lawrence has been tested many times for a twenty-four-year-old. When he was a sophomore at Baylor, his teammate Patrick Dennehy was shot and killed by their teammate Carlton Dotson, and it shook Lawrence up pretty bad. He transferred to Mississippi State, where he struggled with injuries and heartache. But he was still named Southeastern Conference Player of the Year his junior year. The death of his grandfather was a tremendous blow. He idolized my father, and his loss was devastating. Lawrence has stamina, though. He's a strong young man.

Sally-Ann's three children have had to confront the death of their father, Willie, and it has been very hard, especially for Jeremiah. Sally-Ann and Willie adopted Jeremiah after Sally-Ann reported on a story about the difficulty black kids had finding adoptive homes. Sally-Ann took it to heart. Judith, as I've mentioned, is in medical school at Howard University. Kelly is in college in Mississippi. More than any of the other children, Kelly is a true-blue New Orleans girl. I just know she'll be there the rest of her life.

Dorothy's two daughters, Jessica and Lauren, are fine young women, and both are in college. They've had their share of struggle with their parents' divorce after twenty-five years of marriage. But like all of the kids, they are extremely close to their family. My parents' legacy of keeping loved ones close to the heart has spread to the next generation.

Family means everything to me. Often I hear about family rifts, where one person isn't speaking to the other. Grudges grow over insults and grievances that people just can't let go of. It can happen even in the closest families, when the stresses and strains of life set you on edge. Sadly, it can happen at the very times we need one another most. We should be pulling close, yet our angers and resentments can drive us apart.

The most dangerous time for family breakups seems to be around death. Death has a way of shaking the very ground you're standing on, and sometimes what gets shaken loose in the process isn't so pretty.

Like I said, it can happen in even the tightest families. When Grandma Sally died, the whole family went to Ohio for the funeral. Afterward, we gathered in her small apartment. Grandma Sally didn't have much in the way of material possessions, but she had some things of sentimental value, and Mom told us each to take mementoes. I took her copy of *Streams in the Desert*, and then I saw her wedding ring. I decided I should have the ring, because I was the only one of my siblings who wasn't married, and it might be the only wedding ring I ever had.

When Sally-Ann saw me with the ring, she said, "Oh, I wanted that."

I hadn't considered Sally-Ann. "Do you want it?" I asked, not very graciously.

"Oh, no," she said coolly. "You took it. I guess you can have it."

Our parents had arranged to fly home, but the four of us were driving. Butch was at the wheel, and I was beside him in the front seat. Dorothy and Sally-Ann were in back.

As we were driving along, I could hear Sally-Ann mumbling to Dorothy in the backseat. I couldn't catch every word, but I got the gist of it: "*She thinks she's so . . . I'm going to teach my daughters better . . . just took the ring . . .*"

Finally, I got fed up. I turned around and handed Sally-Ann the ring. "You can have it. I don't want it," I said angrily.

Sally-Ann slipped the ring on her finger. "Thank you," she said. We didn't speak again all the way to Mississippi.

When we got to our parents' house at the Pass, where I was being dropped off, we tensely said our good-byes, and I stormed into the house. I was fuming. I was never going to speak to my sister again!

About five minutes later the phone rang. It was Butch. "Robin," he said, with a sternness that was unusual for him, "we are not going to let this happen. Families split up over this kind of thing, and we are not going to let this night end before you two make up." He put Sally-Ann on the phone, and we were both feeling kind of chastened. We said our "I love you's" and "I'm sorry's," and we put an end to the bitter feelings.

I marveled at my brother. Butch rarely raised an issue. Like all the Roberts men, he was strong and quiet. Maybe it had to do with having three sisters and never being able to get a word in edgewise. But when it was important, Butch was a force to be reckoned with.

A week later, Sally-Ann came over to the house with the ring and a beautiful card. "I truly want you to have Grandma Sally's ring," she said. I was very touched. We hugged, and we both knew it wasn't about the darn ring. Today we joke about the incident.

I'd like to tell every person reading this book that if anger or disappointment or resentment has created a rift with a parent or sibling, do what you can to make amends. Maybe you'll have to swallow your pride, and maybe you'll have to give up your feeling of righteousness. But for better or worse, our family is the one thing we have for sure in this life. Do what it takes to keep them close to your heart.

I have had many occasions to reflect about the quality of parenting that gave us such a good start in life. My parents were both very involved in our upbringing. There was one steadfast rule in our household: When the streetlights came on, the Roberts children went home. We were not allowed to play outside at night when we were kids. We always ate supper together at the dinner table by candlelight. It was fun to see who would get to light the candles each night. I thought every family in America ate dinner by candlelight!

My parents did not want to be our best friends. They were very clear about their roles—to guide, teach, and discipline us. My father was the chief disciplinarian, something he accomplished effectively by the sheer power of his presence. All he had to do was clear his throat and we would scatter.

As I mentioned earlier, our home was a no-whine zone. Dad and Mom never pandered to our lower instincts. I remember coming home from a high school basketball game and being very upset. I'd had a rough game, and I'd been kind of a jerk. In the fourth quarter, we were down to the wire, and I committed a silly foul. Just careless. My coach, Ann Logue, called time out, got right in my face, and said, "One more foul and that's it, young lady. You're out of the game." Everyone was staring, and I was embarrassed. But I had an attitude that day that wasn't very sportsmanlike. So I went right back out and fouled as quick as I could.

"That's it!" screamed the coach. "Go home. Get out of here."

I was burning, and I knew I'd screwed up, but by the time I got home I just wanted sympathy. So I kind of whined that the coach made me leave the game, without revealing anything about my own actions.

My parents' immediate response was, "Robin, what did *you* do?" They correctly guessed that my own conduct got me into trouble. I think about this whenever I hear about parents attacking coaches and schools because their children complain about mistreatment. Not that kids aren't sometimes mistreated. But when parents go rushing in with all their protective hackles up, they miss the chance to teach their children important lessons about good sportsmanship and respectful behavior.

Parents don't always realize how much power and influence they have. So many times I hear parents say they don't know how to discipline their kids. But they also want their kids to like them. I remember our parents didn't care one iota what we thought of them. If we didn't want to do something and asked Mom why we had to, she said, "Because I'm the mother, and I said so." And it worked.

We knew the difference between right and wrong, and we knew when we were stepping over the line. We didn't even have to be told. I remember when I was a junior in college, I decided I was going to buy a motorcycle. I knew I should tell someone in my family what I was doing, but no way was that going to be my parents. So I confided in my sister Dorothy. I made her promise that she wouldn't tell Mom and Dad that I was about to buy a motorcycle.

The night before I was going to make my forbidden purchase, the phone rang in my dorm room. It was my mother. She said Dorothy had called and was worried about me. Dorothy had kept her promise and not told my parents the reason for her concern— just that she was concerned. That's all it took. I got up the nerve and boldly told my mom I was buying a motorcycle in the morning. All she said was, "Hold on; here's your father." My dad got on the phone and told me in no uncertain terms that no daughter of his was going to do something so dangerous and foolish. He threatened to take away the car he and my mother had given me to use at school. Still can't believe I conned them—I mean convinced them—that I needed a car on campus. Because I had such respect for my dad I abided by his wishes. But do you know that years later my dad still brought up that incident, worried that he had not handled it correctly. My parents' objective may not have been to become our best friends, but they certainly did. The core values of spirituality and integrity have served me well during all the rough times.

The hardest moment of my life was the day I learned my father had died suddenly. I was on the mat. I didn't know how I would bear not having him in my world. At times like that you need faith more than ever.

Butch, Sally-Ann, Dorothy, and I decided we'd each give a tribute to Dad at the service. The church was packed. Diane, Charlie, Tony Perkins, and other *GMA* colleagues made the trip to Mississippi. It was hard to imagine having the wherewithal to speak, and I don't even remember what I said. But I do remember my quiet brother, the mainstay, stepping up and saying in such a heartfelt way to the congregation, "Thank you, thank you, thank you, for loving my father."

And I remember my mother, who once again provided the model of strength. While the rest of us were in a puddle, she carried herself with such grace. The service was like a celebration—beautiful and uplifting. When it ended, my mother led us out behind the coffin, and we were singing the great gospel song *"When we all get to heaven what a day of rejoicing that will be . . . and we'll sing and shout the victory."* My mother's voice rose above the others. And I realized she truly believed that we were all going to get to heaven, and what a day of rejoicing that will be.

Charlie Gibson told me later, "I've never been to a service like that. It was the most uplifting thing I've ever experienced." I knew what he meant. It was a powerfully comforting event. Afterward, we made our way in a caravan to the military cemetery for the burial. My mom, siblings, and I were in the family car following the hearse. When we made the turn into the cemetery, we looked back and were stunned to see a line of cars as far as the eye could see. Mom squeezed my hand. "Honey, do you see that?" she asked in awe. "Yeah, Mom, I do," I said. She quietly responded, "I'm not talking to you, I'm talking to your father."

The graveside ceremony at a military funeral takes your breath away. The military guard gave a twenty-one-gun salute, the gunfire piercing the air. Then taps was played, and the flag was removed from Dad's coffin, folded, and presented to Mom, "with the thanks of a grateful nation." It was a perfect tribute, but the pain was still there. I've been told that losing a parent is like losing a piece of yourself, and it felt that way to me.

These are the times when you're tested, when your faith may waver, and my mother was and continues to be our rock. She told us that someone had said to her, "You can have sorrowful grief or you can have happy grief," and she was choosing to have happy grief. It made a huge impression on me—the idea that you can choose the kind of grief you have.

My mother is a remarkable woman. I can't say that enough. Right now she's probably on twelve different medications. She's had what are called TIAs—

temporary strokes. She had a knee replacement that did not go well. She's been arthritic for as long as I can remember. She's had numerous surgeries and has high blood pressure, and she just has to be in awful pain sometimes. But you wouldn't know it. She refuses to complain. Just like the little girl who once sang outside her parents' window, she still sees the world as an optimistic place. She has a great sense of herself, of her identity, and she is very independent. She refuses to live with any of her children. She still drives. And she makes a difference to others every day.

My mother has opened my eyes to many realities, including what it is like to be aging in America. I did a series for *GMA* where I literally walked in my mother's shoes. That was the name of the series: "In Their Shoes." We hired the makeup artist who had done such an incredible job for the movie *Shallow Hal*, and he turned forty-five-year-old me into an eight-five-year-old woman. I wore a suit that constrained me so that I moved like a person with arthritis. And when I looked in the mirror I was a little shocked to see not my mother's but my grandmother's face looking back at me. I started crying a little, because it was such a shock. During the series I brought my mother on the show to talk about what it was like to grow older. She was so elegant and inspiring as she spoke about the seasons of our life and that she's now in the winter of her life. And she enjoyed the summer and she enjoyed the spring and now she will enjoy the winter. Her words were very soothing to many of our viewers. And every time she's on the air I am flooded with e-mails and letters of people wanting to talk to her. She still corresponds with some of our viewers. It's really quite remarkable.

It sounds simple, but a positive outlook is a big part of it. It's probably hard to be really successful in life if you're a glass-half-empty type of person. I am inspired daily by my mother's faith and optimism. And I'm certain that my sister Sally-Ann inherited that gene. I am often in awe of her; she's like a rock in the storm. After Katrina, Sally-Ann gave many inspirational speeches. Her theme: "The power is on!" One morning, a woman in the *GMA* studio audience said to me, "I saw your sister speak. She was really something." I grinned. " 'The power is on,' right?" The woman smiled back. "That's right. The power is on."

For me, Sally-Ann epitomizes a particular reflection in *Streams in the Desert* that reminds us: "Great souls have great sorrows . . . great truths are greatly won, not found by chance." That's the way she lives, and it's how she overcame the loss of Willie. Sally-Ann and Willie had been college sweethearts, married for twenty-five years. They were such partners, in every sense of the word. And suddenly, when he was only forty-nine, colon cancer came and swept him away. It wasn't even six months from his diagnosis to his death. And I wondered, how do you go on if you're Sally-Ann? But her faith never wavered.

Faith and family—they're the foundation in good times and bad. I never take for granted the upbringing I had. I'm very appreciative. I know I can trust my instincts because they developed in me as a result of positive experiences and teaching. But I'm also aware that I can't just blithely tell someone to "go with your gut," because that person's gut may have been honed through fear and feelings of inadequacy.

Not everyone has a family to support them. And if you don't have a family, create one. You *can* pick your family—because what are true friends but family? I have also been incredibly blessed by my close circle of friends. Sometimes it awes me that of the billions of people on the planet, you can find those few who become an unconditional support system.

With true friends, you can be yourself. If you have to pretend to be someone different, if you have to mask your feelings and your flaws, if you're always trying to look good to impress your friends, here's a news flash. They're not friends.

When I was growing up, my parents were harder on me about my friends than almost anything else in my life. They understood the concept of peer pressure before it became a catchphrase. They would grill me: *Who are they? What do their parents do? Are they good students? Do they go to church? Do they smoke?* I was impatient with the questions then. Now I understand.

It turns out my circle of friends were pretty solid citizens—Cheryl Antoine, Luella Fairconeture, and Pat Barnes, my mixed-doubles partner. We just gravitated to one another. None of us smoked or drank. And it just so happens that we were all from stable, loving families.

My friend Pat Barnes was greatly influenced by Dad. He always said that he was a little awestruck the first time he came over to our house and met him. He thought being an Air Force colonel was the coolest thing. And guess what? Pat is now a full colonel in the Air Force, stationed at the Pentagon. I have to say, though, in high school Pat would probably have been voted least likely to become a colonel and a family man. I always thought my dad planted a seed in him, and that seed grew. There was a bittersweet aspect to Pat's promotion, though. It came shortly after Hurricane Katrina. Pat called and asked if he could have Dad's eagles pinned on him. It would have been so poetic—and Dad would have been honored. But we had lost the eagles in the storm. Still, I know Pat was thinking about Dad that day.

Today, I continue to be blessed with a tremendous group of friends. I know they're watching my back. If a reviewer or commentator writes anything unflattering about me, they're on the phone: "Don't pay any attention. That person doesn't know you." They keep me sane.

At my father's funeral, I looked up and there were my closest friends—Tara, Jo, Kim, Loisann, Julie, Scarlett, Nancy, Michelle, Beth, Nell, Richlyn. They flew in from California to Connecticut and everywhere in between to be with me when I needed them most. Driving to the cemetery, I thought, they should be in the family car with me, because they *are* family.

My friends and I have had some great times and some wild vacations. We've also had some rough times, but we're solid. Women have a gift for friendship that often eludes men. When I'm with my women friends, nothing is out of bounds. If you had a humiliating experience, you'll talk about it without fear—and probably end up laughing. Men are sometimes too careful with one another, not wanting to show too much emotion or vulnerability. I think they could learn something about friendship from women.

Our culture today so easily promotes the superficial, the material, and the false. Yet if you look around, the people with the greatest wealth and fame are often those with shaky family lives, addiction problems, and struggles with depression. Whether you have material success or not, true success is not possible if you lack an inner life. I am a person of faith, and that faith sustains me. It is a positive, uniting force. Too often these days people use faith in a divisive way— to hold themselves up as better than others and to condemn those who don't share their beliefs. The faith I learned at my parents' feet was a faith of compassion and service. It's a faith that embraces all kinds of people.

Religion has become the elephant in the room in this country. People are kind of afraid of it, and assumptions have grown about one political party being the party of faith and the other being the party of non-faith. I remember interviewing Senator Barak Obama on this subject. He had decided to try to break through the logjam and create a place for dialogue. Senator Obama told me, "We have to make sure that we don't get so locked into a particular perception about how one party or the other thinks, that we miss the enormous complexity and diversity of religious views all across the country." He cited examples of evangelicals who are committed to protecting the environment, and other folks who are dedicated to helping the poor. These are potential bridges where we can begin having conversations with one another, instead of loud political battles. As I spoke with Senator Obama, I imagined how powerful it would be if we used our faith as an open channel instead of a closed door—if we remembered that we all have more in common than we have differences.

For me, faith is the voice that is always with me, urging me to make a difference in the world in a positive way. I believe that whatever your religion or spiritual beliefs, every person can strive to live a life of meaning.

I remember how my awareness of this was heightened long ago, when I was a college student. Early one morning when I was leaving my dorm room at Southeastern I ran into a fellow student. She was a young woman whom many people avoided because she would constantly talk to you about religion. Not a very popular subject among many college students—especially those who were majoring in partying.

But that morning, even though I was late for work I stopped to talk to her. She had a large poster board and had drawn a long, straight line on it. She asked me, "How long do you expect to live?" Good genes run in my family, so I told her, "Ninety to ninety-five years." She then handed me a marker and asked me to put a dot on the line at the point I thought represented ninety-five years.

I had no idea what she was up to. I placed my dot about a quarter of the way from the beginning of the line. She then told me to look at all the remaining space on the poster board. Huh? I'll never forget what she said next: "Robin, how are you going to live your ninety-five years on this earth so you can enjoy eternity?" I was absolutely speechless. I could not answer her. I was just frozen in thought.

I had heard countless sermons about that subject in my life, but it had never before been illustrated to me in such a powerful way. From that moment on I made a conscious decision to do things that would enrich my life, not things that would make me rich.

For me success goes beyond making a lot of money or being on TV every day. In the end these are small things that mean nothing if I am not striving toward personal enrichment and making an effort to live a life with meaning.

That is why every day I ask God for grace. Grace is the infinite love and mercy shown to others. It keeps me humble in the awareness of my small place in the world, and it fills me with gratitude that I have been so unaccountably blessed. Grace helps me see the goodness in all different types of people, and it helps me maintain serenity in the face of insults to my ego, or weariness, or conflict. I can't predict what tomorrow will bring, and I don't try. Life is lived in the present, so when I ask for grace each morning, it's not for tomorrow or next week—just for the present day. I don't try to get ahead of myself. And you know what? When tomorrow comes, I'll ask for grace tomorrow.

8. Make Your Mess Your Message

Remember when I said: "Isn't it wonderful how life can surprise you?" I never thought I'd write a book, but I did. And I never thought I would be diagnosed with breast cancer. But that's exactly what happened just a few months after the release of the book.

I was enjoying my summer. Traveling around the country meeting folks and asking them their rules to live by. I was about to leave for a rare two-week vacation when my beloved colleague and friend, Joel Siegel, lost his battle with colon cancer. I delayed my trip so I could attend Joel's funeral. It was a beautiful service, filled with wonderful stories of Joel's strength and courage. We also laughed a lot. Joel had a terrific sense of humor, and the laughter soothed our broken hearts.

Right after the service I headed to Key West to begin my vacation with dear friends. It was a delightful week full of sun and plenty of fun, but Joel was never far from my mind. We decided to have a tribute show for him on *Good Morning America* a week after his passing. I had hopped out to San Diego to deliver a commencement address, so I caught a red-eye and flew back overnight so I could be there.

Many of our former colleagues joined Diane and me to remember Joel. Former *GMA* hosts David Hartman and Joan Lunden were there, along with former *GMA* weatherman Spencer Christian, and, of course, Charlie Gibson. They had all worked with Joel and become good friends over the years. I did a piece about Joel's courageous battle with colon cancer, including his own reflections, taped when he was alive. Joel spoke about how hard it was to hear from his doctor that if he had gotten a colonoscopy at the age of fifty instead of fifty-three, the outcome might have been different. As he fought his own illness, Joel made it his mission to encourage people to have regular cancer screenings.

After the show, I lingered to talk with our medical editor, Dr. Tim Johnson. I was angry that cancer had taken Joel. "How many people have to die before we *do* something about this awful disease?" I demanded. "So much money has been invested in fighting cancer, so much time has been spent—but where do we stand?" I wanted answers. Tim assured me that great and significant medical advances were being made, but that we also had to do our part. We must be diligent when it comes to our own health care, especially screening for early detection. I knew he was right, but to tell you the truth, it didn't really hit home.

That very night I discovered something that would change my life. I had driven to Connecticut to resume the last week of my vacation. Exhausted from my all-night flight and the emotional drain of the show, I fell asleep on the couch. I woke up much later and sleepily started changing into my pj's. And then I stopped. I felt a lump in my right breast. I immediately assumed that it was probably a pulled muscle from my awkward position on the couch.

The next morning I woke up and immediately

gave myself a breast self-exam. The lump was still there. For a moment I froze. What should I do? I didn't really have a family doctor. I e-mailed Diane and asked her if she could recommend someone. I also reached out to my colleague and friend, Deborah Roberts. She referred me to a doctor who agreed to see me when I returned to New York the following week. I tried my best to enjoy the remainder of my vacation, but Joel was really resonating in my heart now. I kept thinking about his message of early detection.

Monday morning, July 16, I was back on the air at *GMA*. That afternoon I went to Dr. Albert Knapp for a general checkup. Now, here's the crazy part. I didn't mention the lump. Maybe I thought if I didn't tell him about it, it wouldn't exist. Dr. Knapp gave me an examination and took my family history. He had a warm, easygoing nature that put me at ease. I felt as if I'd been going to him for years. But no mention of a lump, and why would there be since I hadn't mentioned my concern to him?

However, just as Dr. Knapp was about to leave the examining room, I stopped him. "Dr. Knapp, before you go, could you please check out this lump I have? I'm sure it's nothing." My voice was shaking.

Unbelievable—I'd almost chickened out! Here I was, doing the right thing, being diligent about my health care, but I had to force myself to speak up. I guess that sometimes the unknown is less fearful than the known—or at least it feels that way.

Dr. Knapp gave me a breast exam and felt the lump. He immediately ordered a mammogram and an ultrasound. I walked a couple of blocks to the radiology center. Luckily, it was the end of the day and they told me if I could wait they would squeeze me in. I've heard countless stories of others having to wait months for a routine mammogram. But I'm told if you have a lump, most places around the country will make an exception and see you in a more timely fashion. Remember what I said earlier about being patient and persistent. That is especially true when it comes to your health.

My mammogram came back normal. It was fortunate that Dr. Knapp had also ordered the ultrasound. As the technician was performing it, Dr. Mona Darwish, the attending physician, watched the screen. Dr. Darwish had an extensive background in breast cancer work, and her trained eye picked up a tumor that had not been detected with the mammogram. I later learned that is quite common to get a clean mammogram but discover a tumor on the ultrasound. This is especially true for young women whose denser breast tissue makes it harder to detect abnormalities. It is recommended that younger women and those with a high risk for breast cancer have ultrasounds. Of course, I see the wisdom of that now.

Dr. Darwish told me she wanted to do a core biopsy. It was late in the day and I was tired and hungry. I just wanted to leave. I asked her if we could do it another time. She gently squeezed my hand and said, "Why don't we just take care of this right now." I think she could sense that if I got off that examining table, I wouldn't be coming back anytime soon. In fact, the next day I was headed to Atlanta on assignment. The rest of my week was jam-packed. I had a lot of catching up to do after being on vacation for two weeks. The excuses were my feeble effort to mask my fear. Once again, it felt easier to just not know.

Dr. Darwish was persistent. I had the feeling that she wasn't going to take no for an answer, so I agreed to have the biopsy. I'm not going to lie to you. The biopsy was not the most pleasant experience. I'm not exactly crazy about needles—especially one being inserted into my breast! I was relieved when it was over. Dr. Darwish said the results should be back by the end of the next day.

After *GMA* the following morning, I flew to Atlanta. As the plane pulled up to the gate, I turned on my BlackBerry and cell phone. There was an e-mail from my assistant, Ayana, saying that Dr. Knapp's office had called, and I needed to answer my cell phone because he would be trying to reach me. I'd just finished reading Ayana's message when my phone rang. It was Dr. Knapp. I was still sitting on the plane when he gave me the test results. "Robin, it's cancer." I'm sure he said more, but all I heard was "*Blah, blah, blah . . . CANCER . . . blah, blah, blah.*" I do remember agreeing to have a breast MRI the next day in New York and to meet with a breast surgeon.

In the movies, when you learn you have cancer, you are sitting in the doctor's office holding a loved one's hand. I was all alone, about to get off a plane in Atlanta. I had boarded in New York as *just Robin*. Now I was *Robin . . . with breast cancer*. My eyes started to fill with tears, and I put on sunglasses so no one would notice.

A driver was waiting to take me to Pine Mountain,

Georgia. I wanted to call my family and friends to let them know I had cancer. But I didn't want the driver to know what was going on because I wasn't ready for the public to learn about my diagnosis. He was a very nice man, but a bit inquisitive, and I knew he'd be listening. So I played a little guessing game with my loved ones. "Remember how I told you I was going to have that thing checked out?" I asked, and in a quivering voice added, "What do you think I found out?" I guess my tone was a dead giveaway. They knew. They'd been praying for the best, but were prepared for the worst, and here it was. Cancer.

What is so remarkable about that day is that in the midst of being scared and shaking with my personal crisis, I could become so uplifted and inspired by bearing witness to someone else's tragedy. I was in Pine Mountain to interview Michael and Jeri Bishop, whose only son, Jamie, had been killed months earlier in the horrific shootings that took place at Virginia Tech. Jamie had been a beloved teacher there, and his parents were still numb with grief. Nevertheless, they had agreed to talk to me for a story that would air the first day the students returned to Tech.

The Bishops were lovely people. They welcomed

me into their home and fed me delicious cherries. Their warmth touched me, and I wanted to fall into their arms and cry, "I have cancer." But I pulled myself together. They had lost their son in one of the most tragic ways imaginable. *I* was there to comfort *them*.

The Bishops spoke so eloquently and movingly about Jamie. When I asked them what they wanted the students returning to Tech to know, Jeri said, "I want them to know that they are in the right place at the right time." Her comment was in reference to President Bush's words during a memorial service that the thirty-two people killed were in the wrong place at the wrong time. The Bishops felt their incredible son was where he was supposed to be. He was a passionate teacher making a difference in countless young lives.

I hugged the Bishops good-bye and got back in the car to return to the airport. I was desperate for some privacy. All I wanted was to get home. But my flight was delayed, and it was almost 11:00 p.m. before I walked through my front door. I collapsed on my couch and had a good long cry.

I was feeling so many emotions. I was scared, angry, confused, and even embarrassed. How could I have cancer? I prided myself on being health-conscious and athletic. Would people think I had done something wrong? Did *I* think I had done something wrong? A million questions raced through my bewildered mind, and none of them had answers.

The next day I had a breast MRI and met with my surgeon, Dr. Lauren Cassell. In a word, she's phenomenal. She clearly explained the situation to me. My tumor appeared to be a little more than two centimeters. During surgery she would also check my lymph nodes. She assured me that my prognosis was very good. My breast was swollen and slightly bruised from the biopsy. (I told you I don't like needles!) So we would have to wait a few weeks before she could operate.

When I told Diane, she swung into immediate action. Diane and I have always been close. We call ourselves Thelma and Louise, and some mornings we feel like we're in that convertible about to go over a cliff. We've always been there for each other. When my beloved father passed away, Diane was in our front yard in Mississippi the next morning. We were backing out of the driveway to go to the funeral home to make arrangements and almost ran over her.

She had stopped at one of my family's favorite restaurants on the coast, Mary Mahoney's, to get us some gumbo. I can't tell you what it meant to my family and to me for Diane to travel all that way to give us such loving support. It's something I will never forget.

Diane was there for me again after my diagnosis. She called numerous doctors and experts in the field. Part of the reason that Diane is a stellar journalist is because of her inquisitive nature. Her thirst for answers and information is unparalleled. She is also one of the most compassionate and loving people that I have ever known. She knew I wasn't sleeping well at night because I couldn't stop thinking. I was afraid that I'd missed something. So Diane would call me and say, "You can get some rest. Your shift is over. I'm on watch now."

I had to make a decision about whether to go public with my diagnosis. It was so personal—I longed to maintain that zone of privacy. I dreaded the prospect that people would treat me differently if they knew. I wanted to keep things as normal as possible. Then again, what was normal now?

A few days before my surgery, after giving it a lot

of thought and talking it over with Diane, I decided that I would tell the *GMA* audience. The main reason was that our viewers are truly like our extended family, and I had felt their love and concern in poignant ways. They had mourned the death of my father with me. They had cried along with me when my hometown was virtually destroyed by Hurricane Katrina. I knew I could trust them with this new pain, and I didn't want them to hear about my diagnosis from anyone but us. My voice was trembling with emotion when I declared on air, "I have breast cancer." Diane could tell I was about to lose it, and she reached over and gently held my hand. That helped me regain my composure, and we continued to talk to our viewers—our family—as if they were sitting in our living room.

It wasn't just about me. We tried to use the show to educate people and encourage them to seek early detection. We dispelled the myth that most people who are diagnosed with breast cancer have a family history of the disease. There's no history in my family. In fact, over 80 percent of people who are diagnosed with breast cancer have no prior family history. Eighty percent! We also discussed the fact that my tumor was not detected by a mammogram but by an ultrasound. I said how blessed I was to have discovered it early.

Diane ended our discussion by saying, "The woman who gave us seven rules to live by has demonstrated every one of them." I quickly added, "I now have an eighth rule. Early detection." But the real eighth rule, which I would call upon time and again in the coming months, was an old saying from my mother: *Make your mess your message.*

The reaction to my announcement was immediate and overwhelming. Calls and e-mails started pouring in to ABC. People wanted to comfort me. They also wanted to let us know that because of what Diane and I said on the show, they were going to be more diligent about their own health care. In fact, the ABC station in New York did a story later that same day about a woman who went to have a mammogram after hearing our discussion.

By the time I reached my office a couple of hours after the show, the calls were pouring in there, too. Ayana was amazing in the way she handled the avalanche. She knew I was not expecting this reaction and wasn't fully prepared to discuss my situation with everyone. The last thing I wanted was to spend hours on the phone talking. But after I'd been in my office for a half hour, Ayana appeared in the doorway. "I think this is a call you *will* want to take," she said.

"Who is it?" I asked, feeling tired.

"Elizabeth Edwards." Elizabeth Edwards had first been diagnosed with cancer at the end of the 2004 election season, when her husband John was a vice-presidential running mate for John Kerry. Now John Edwards was running for president, and Elizabeth had bravely announced to the world that her breast cancer had returned—and she was determined to keep fighting.

I picked up the phone. "Mrs. Edwards, thanks so much for calling," I said, genuinely touched.

"Please, Robin, call me Elizabeth," she replied. It felt as if she were holding my hand through the phone. She wanted me to know that she understood what I was feeling, the uncertainty of what was ahead of me, and also how difficult it was to go public. She told me that she was very glad that I had decided to share my diagnosis with the viewers, and that by doing so I might have saved lives. It was an enlightening and incredibly helpful conversation. Elizabeth officially welcomed me to the "sisterhood" of breast cancer survivors. Because the moment you are diagnosed, you are a survivor.

That night, for the first time since I learned I had cancer, I slept like a baby. I know this may sound odd, but I actually *felt* the prayers that were being said for me that night. It's hard to explain, but I had an over-whelming sense that the healing had truly begun.

On August 3, I finally had surgery. It was a partial mastectomy, and some lymph nodes were removed. My family was gathered in the waiting room. My sister Sally-Ann had printed out a batch of the e-mails viewers had sent me. She patiently read them and put a big "S" on those from survivors. Their stories moved us all, and they would continue to inspire me in the months to come.

The following days were just a blur. I was allowed to go home and recuperate—but mostly what I did was wait. Although every indication was that the cancer had not spread, I had to wait for confirmation.

Sally-Ann and Dorothy returned home a few days after the surgery, and Butch arrived to help Mom take care of me. They watched over me like a hawk and wouldn't let me out of their sight. One day, we ventured out for lunch and stopped at a drugstore to pick up a few things. I begged my brother and mom to let me go in by myself. I was tired of this watchful entourage. But wouldn't you know it, while I was in the store my cell phone rang. It was my doctor. I stood stock still in the aisle and waited for the verdict. Good news and bad news. There was still no indication the cancer had spread, but it was more aggressive than previously thought. The initial diagnosis was DCIS—ductal carcinoma in situ—a noninvasive form of breast cancer. But under the microscope the tumor looked "nasty." I had an image of the tumor snarling beneath the glass. The cancer was not DCIS; it was an invasive carcinoma. My doctor told me I would need chemotherapy. By the time I made it back to the car, I was a mess.

Butch and my mom must have thought, "We let you out of our sight for one minute and you come back in tears." They asked me what had happened, but all I could do was sit in the backseat and cry. They patiently waited for me to compose myself, and I told them what my doctor had said. They didn't flinch, but I knew they were worried.

When you hear the word "chemotherapy," you automatically think the worst. *I'm going to lose my hair, I'm going to constantly throw up . . . I may die.* It was the first time since my diagnosis that I seriously contemplated that. *I may die.*

Diane burned up the phone lines calling cancer experts all across the country. I had a number of conversations with Dr. Tim Johnson. You may know him as ABC's longtime medical editor. I know him as a compassionate friend. Tim is always there when anyone in the ABC family needs him. If you stub your toe, Dr. Tim is there for you. Tim is knowledgeable, but he also has an unmistakable spirit about him. When I talked to him shortly after my diagnosis in July he told me to be prepared for the possibility of chemo. At the time, my doctors felt that only radiation would be necessary.

But now I was facing chemotherapy, which would be followed by six and a half weeks of radiation. I was completely upfront with ABC executives. Unfortunately, they had recently been down this road. Before we lost Joel Siegel, we were stunned by the death of our beloved anchor, Peter Jennings. He died in 2005 due to complications from lung cancer.

ABC News president David Westin was wonderful. He didn't talk to me as an employee, but rather as a dear friend. David assured me he would see that I had whatever I needed. Bob Iger, president and CEO of our parent company, Walt Disney, personally told me the same thing. Anne Sweeney, president of the Disney-ABC Television Group, took me to lunch to assure me that I had their full support.

What a comfort to know the company you work for gets it—gets that who you are is far more important than what you do. So many cancer patients have told me they were afraid to tell their employers for fear of losing their jobs. It's hard to believe that any company would abandon an employee when she needed them the most. Fortunately, that was one thing I didn't have to worry about.

I returned to *GMA* ten days after my surgery. I was still quite sore, but I wanted to get back to work. I needed my routine to help keep my mind off what was ahead of me. When I walked into my dressing room, it was filled with balloons, flowers, and colorful signs of encouragement. My colleagues had organized a happy homecoming. How blessed I was!

I met with my oncologist, Dr. Ruth Oratz, to set up a schedule for my chemotherapy. I was still feeling resistant to the very idea. I was a person who worked out five times a week and ate a healthy diet. I just couldn't wrap my mind around the idea of putting poison in my body. I questioned Dr. Oratz—did I really need chemo? She assured me that I did. "It's like that fire in your fireplace," she explained. "You know there are a couple of embers in there that, if you poke, could start up a fire again and burn down the whole house. We don't want that to happen. So if we throw water into the fireplace, we put out all those embers. That's what chemotherapy does."

She told me I would need eight rounds of chemo, administered every two weeks. I was determined to continue working as much as possible. I boldly told her, "I want to have the chemo on Friday, after the show, and be back sitting next to Diane on Monday." Dr. Oratz, one of the kindest doctors I have ever known, gently told me that might not be the best idea. My body would need more time to rest.

Dr. Oratz's wisdom was proved when I started the treatments. Chemotherapy is a roller-coaster ride. There's really no way to prepare for it. Everyone's body is different, so there is no typical experience. My veins are small, so a port was implanted in my chest. The chemo was administered through the port. I had eight treatments—four Adriamycin (AC) and four Taxol. I called AC the "red devil." It's red and administered in a syringe. I just wanted to grab the syringe and smash it with my bare hands.

I had been advised to visit different chemotherapy rooms before I made my decision on which facility to choose. One of the reasons I chose Dr. Oratz is because she only treats patients with breast cancer. Her office is not in a hospital. It's an intimate, warm setting. The chemo rooms are small and hold a maximum of two patients at a time. I visited some places (with equally fabulous reputations) that were huge, cold, sterile environments to me. I went with cozy.

My mother was with me for my first two chemo treatments. If she was nervous, she wasn't letting on. Mom settled into the chair next to me and pulled out some material she had received from the Susan G. Komen foundation. She began asking Dr. Oratz questions: What type of chemo would I be receiving today? What were the side effects? What medication would I receive for nausea? During her barrage of questions, I had to leave the room for a moment.

When I was barely outside, I heard my mom quietly ask Dr. Oratz, "As the mother, is there anything you want to tell me that Robin shouldn't know?" No matter how old we are, in our moms' eyes we will always be their children.

I was never in any discomfort when I received chemo. Didn't feel a thing. The hardest part was sitting still for the several hours it took. Family and friends traveled from all across the country to sit with me and help pass the time. My favorite gift came from a close group of friends. It was a shuffle iPod. They'd downloaded photos of us that had been taken over the years—wonderful images of my friends and me laughing, having fun at parties, on vacations, or just hanging out. They also downloaded inspirational songs. So as I was taking chemo, I watched the beautiful video slide show and listened to songs that lifted my spirit. There was lots of Motown (my favorite), like "Ain't No Mountain High Enough." The first song on the play list was "Jesus Take the Wheel." I have to admit I cried my eyes out the first time I heard it. Listening to that iPod, seeing the pictures scroll across the small screen, made it seem like my dear friends were right there in the chemo room with me every time—holding my hand, drying my tears.

I was told to expect to start losing my hair after the second treatment. Weeks earlier I had gone to wig-makers with my stylist, Petula. We settled on Bitz-n-Pieces in New York. It is an exceptional shop. For decades they have tenderly helped people cope with hair loss. I also had a wig made by Raffaele Mollica. He too has lovingly guided people through the most dramatic times in their lives. The wigs were styled to look just like my hair. I was ready. Or so I thought. It's one thing to accept that you're going to lose your hair. It's another thing to experience it.

Right on schedule, a few days after my second chemo, my hair started falling out in large pieces. It was a Sunday. My mom was in the kitchen making dinner. I went into my bathroom and stared in the mirror, and then collapsed on the floor crying uncontrollably. It was such a gut-wrenching moment. Finally, I pulled myself together and went into the kitchen. My mom was by the stove preparing her legendary collard greens. I began to cry again on Mom's shoulder. She sweetly comforted me with one arm as she stirred the greens with the other. She didn't want me too close to the pot!

The next day I met Petula at her salon. I took off my baseball cap and she wondered what all the fuss was about. I still had lots of hair. I sat in her chair and she touched a section of my hair. It fell out right in her hand. In the mirror I could see Petula's eyes grow wide with horror. But without missing a beat, in her soothing Island accent, Petula said, as she always does: "No problem, Robin, no problem."

My mom was returning to Mississippi the next day, and I didn't want to shave my head until she had gone. I thought that the sight of her baby girl completely bald would be too much for her. After she left, Petula and I went to Raffaele's shop. The plan was that Petula would shave my head there so Raffaele could complete the fitting for my wig.

I wasn't sure if this was something I wanted to share with *GMA* viewers. But just in case, I asked photographer Michael Rose to videotape me. We have become friends over the years and I knew Michael and his sound man, Claudio, would handle the situation sensitively. Janice Johnston, one of my many talented colleagues, was there as a producer and friend.

As Petula began clipping my hair, I was filled with so many emotions. I just kept saying over and over, "So much change, so much change." And that's how I felt. So much was changing in my life. So much had changed since my diagnosis only a couple of months earlier. Finally, Petula pulled out the electric clippers. I'll never forget that buzzing sound. But as I brushed the falling hair out of my eyes and stared into the mirror, I didn't see tears. I saw strength. Cancer had already taken so much from me, but now I was in control. I was the one who decided this was the day I would lose all my hair. Not cancer, not chemo, ME!

There are some chemotherapy treatments that do not cause you to lose your hair. I was virtually assured that I would because of AC. I strongly urge anyone who is told this to be preemptive and shave your head. Save yourself the heartache of waiting for your hair to fall out and then slowly watching it do so.

About a month later, I decided to show the video on *GMA. People* magazine had done a feature article on my battle against cancer, and I had allowed them to photograph me without my wig. I didn't want people to be shocked when they saw it, or to think I had been hiding my baldness. I wore the wig on *GMA* because I didn't want my baldness to distract from the stories I was covering. But now I felt that my baldness and all it represented could become the story—another way of reaching out to others who faced cancer. I was determined to make my mess my message.

I was absolutely stunned by the reaction to my video diary. The outpouring of support was once again overwhelming. The countless people who had traveled this path before me knew how personal this was. Many people going through chemo don't want anyone to know they've lost their hair. They have every right to keep it to themselves. There's no right or wrong way. But I wanted to make a statement that I wasn't ashamed to have cancer or to be bald.

Not long after my video diary aired, I ran into a woman at Bitz-n-Pieces. Both of us were bringing in our wigs for a tune-up. She said I had given her the strength to talk to her friends and colleagues about her illness. I was thrilled for her because I knew she was now opening herself up to a source of great comfort. She said she had hidden her illness from them for fear they would treat her differently. But her friends had seen that I was still able to work, and that gave her the courage to speak openly.

Midway through my treatments, I traveled with First Lady Laura Bush to the Middle East. Mrs. Bush has a family history of breast cancer. She personally invited me to accompany her on a portion of a breast cancer awareness initiative with the Komen Foundation. I couldn't pass up this opportunity. My doctors cleared me to travel—although getting my mom's blessing was far more difficult. I spent time with Mrs. Bush in Abu Dhabi and Dubai in the UAE, and Riyadh, Saudi Arabia. I met some incredible women on the trip. Breast cancer is the number-one killer of women in the UAE. Many succumb because the stigma surrounding the disease in that part of the world prevents them from seeking early detection.

The day after I returned from the Middle East, I was back in the chemo chair. The trip was a worthwhile experience but it took a toll on my body. This chemo series was very hard on me. I normally missed only a couple of days of work following treatment. This time I was out for a week. I was achy all over and felt horrible.

I kept a journal to write down the details of how I was feeling after treatments. It helped me to notice patterns. The first couple of days after chemo I was okay. The third day was typically my worst day. I was queasy, but never got sick to my stomach. I did get mouth sores. Biotene toothpaste and mouthwash helped a lot. Sucking on hard candy, especially crystallized ginger, was also helpful. Plus, I drank a great deal of water. I didn't want to become dehydrated.

Chemo also brought on early menopause. So I had the added bonus of dealing with hot flashes. What a joy that was. I was frequently bloated and my skin was sensitive to the touch. I had sounds and smells coming out of me that made me think of my dearly departed dad. My fingertips and toes were numb. My sense of smell was off the charts. I could tell you what my neighbor down the hall was having for dinner. My taste buds were nonexistent. I constantly had a metallic taste in my mouth, so I used plastic utensils to eat. Not that I had much of an appetite.

My skin was as dry as the Sahara Desert. Before applying my makeup, Elena put Vaseline on my face so the makeup had something to stick to. She penciled in my missing eyebrows and glued on eyelashes where mine used to be. It was like putting Humpty Dumpty back together again every morning.

I was thrilled when the day of my last chemo

treatment finally arrived. After *GMA*, my colleagues surprised me by lining up on either side of the hallway from the studio to my dressing room. They had made signs of encouragement and congratulations. They were cheering their heads off. Have I mentioned how much I love my *GMA* family?

Seeing them cheering like that reminded me of the times they gave me videotapes they made of themselves telling jokes. Or should I say *trying* to tell jokes. All in an effort to lift my spirits during chemo. Which they did every time. Especially when I heard Sam Champion's booming laugh. I also remembered the morning Chris Cuomo asked me what I needed most at that moment. I told him "a new pair of legs; mine are killing me from the chemo." Wouldn't you know that when I walked into my dressing room after the show that day, a new pair of legs was waiting for me. Chris found some shapely mannequin legs!

Dr. Oratz's team has a wonderful tradition. At the end of the last chemo session, the nurses dance around you, blowing bubbles. The amazing Beth, who had worked with me the most, was leading the way, saying: "Each bubble represents a good wish for you." I watched the bubbles cascading over me like blessings.

Shortly after I completed chemo, Diane, Chris, Sam, and I decided to challenge each other. To dare each other to venture outside of our comfort zones. My challenge was to be a model during New York City's Fashion Week. As you can imagine, I was feeling less than fashionable at the time. Chemo left me bald and bloated and looking like anything but a model. Fashion icon Tyra Banks was kind enough to teach me how to walk like a model. Isaac Mizrahi dressed me in one of his fabulous gowns and graciously invited me to walk in his show...live on *GMA*! That morning as I was preparing backstage with the other young, gorgeous models (including a former winner of *America's Next Top Model*), I had on my trusty wig. But before I took the catwalk, I decided to take it off. I said to myself: "This is who you are, Robin. Embrace it." I held my bald head high and strutted my stuff. Later people told me they cheered me on and cried when they saw me do that. Many told me they thought of a loved one who had lost their battle with cancer. One e-mail I received touched me in particular. A mother told me she was watching that morning with her young child. He wanted to know why I didn't have any hair. She told him that because I was sick, I had to take medicine and it made my hair fall out. Her young son told her, "I still think she's pretty." The mom thanked me for helping her teach her son a valuable lesson about life. Make your mess your message!

As elated as I was to finish chemo, I still had a long way to go. About a month later, I began my radiation treatments. I was exhausted by now. My knees and back were killing me. For the first time, my white blood cell count dropped. I began looking for non-traditional therapies to support me.

Sheryl Crow, who is a breast cancer survivor, told me about her nutritionist, Rachel Beller. This woman is a dynamo. She is passionate about helping and educating people about proper nutrition. Rachel told me I needed more protein in my diet during radiation. She was also very big on fiber. I was serious about taking her advice.

In addition, I went to an acupuncturist for the first time. I was, of course, apprehensive about the needles. But I soon learned I didn't need to be. Dr. Wang's expertise brought much-needed relief to my sore body. I liked the idea of combining Eastern and Western medicines.

My white blood cell count improved and I continued on with radiation. Every day after *GMA*, I headed across town for my treatment. The technicians, Tina, Suzy, and Jacqui, were always upbeat, and they had music playing for patients to listen to during radiation. Seeing them every day for almost two months helped me get through it. We formed a sweet bond. They would input my information into a computer. Carefully position me on the table. Line up the small tattoos that had been placed on my chest with rays of light. The whole process took only five minutes.

My radiation oncologist, Dr. Roberto Lipsztein, examined me once a week. He's Brazilian and has a zest for life. He would check to see how my body was handling the radiation. Because of my skin color, I didn't suffer any burning until late in my treatment. It was like having a sunburn. A really bad sunburn. But the side effect that bothered me the most was fatigue. I just couldn't shake it. I had been able to lightly exercise a couple of days a week during chemo, but I just didn't have the strength to work out during radiation.

I started to feel depressed. My body was like a stranger to me. My mind at times felt like mush. It was hard to concentrate or focus. I could only manage to sleep a few hours at a time. I was sick and tired of feeling sick and tired.

I had to get quiet and remind myself that I had gotten through hard times before. Remind myself of my own rules to live by. I summoned them up, using them to buttress my flagging spirits.

Even though my knees were shaking, I had taken the shot. I had been scared to tell Dr. Knapp about my lump, but I had. And now I was receiving the care that would save my life.

My big dream is to be cancer free, but I am focusing on the small things that will get me there. If for some reason the treatment I have received does not succeed, I will dive back in and find something that will. I will never stop fighting.

I will not play the "cancer card." I will not use cancer as an excuse for not achieving the goals I have set for myself. Cancer forced me out of my comfort zone. But as I stated previously, "There *is* no comfort zone. Life comes at us in ways we can't predict or control." I know that now more than ever. I am focusing on the solution, not the problem. I don't dwell on the fact that I have cancer. I spend my energy and resources on conquering this disease.

My faith, family, and friends have never been closer to my heart. Do you realize how humbling it is to know you are constantly being lifted up in prayer? Countless people, of all religions, have told me they are praying for me. Thank you all and I love you back.

There are not enough pages to convey my gratitude to my family and friends. Tears are streaming down my face as I write this, thinking about their unconditional love. Words seem so inadequate.

I was asked to write an entire book about my experience with cancer. I respectfully declined. Cancer is no more than a chapter in my life. And it will not be the last chapter.

One Final Thought . . .

Now that I've given you my rules, I want you to go out and break them. Then write your own. Because when it comes right down to it, there is no playbook for your own unique, wonderful life. Ultimately, you've got to live it for yourself. And whatever your dream, you've got to want it for yourself. Come to think of it, that old high school sports cheer rings as true in life as it does in basketball.

You gotta want it
To win it
So come on strong!

If you want it bad enough, and it comes from the heart, you can do anything—even when you're tired or discouraged or scared.

The main reason I wrote this book was that after Hurricane Katrina I was just feeling so helpless and hopeless. And then I experienced the outpouring of passion and compassion. The steady stream of volunteers. The people who put their lives on hold to help complete strangers. They lifted me up, and I was reminded again of how very blessed I am. What a feeling. I wanted everyone to have that incredible feeling of knowing they're living the life they want.

It's hard sometimes, because life doesn't always feel so good. There are sad times and tragedies and moments of doubt when it's hard to pick yourself up. What then?

I was mulling over that very thing one day not long ago, when I came upon the answer in the most unlikely place—the makeup room at *GMA*.

As I've said, makeup is definitely not my favorite thing. I hate having to sit still for my hour in the chair, especially at five in the morning. But my Team

Beauty can make it all worthwhile. Eleana and Petula have been with me since I became an anchor at *GMA*. In addition to their skills (which I put to the test every morning), they happen to be incredibly spiritual women. Every day they greet me with an affirmation for the day, and it perks me right up. I find that I really do carry it around in my head. So on that particular day they hit me with this one:

> *You have to change the way you think*
> *in order to change the way you feel.*

As I sat in my makeup chair, I started to chant it— *You have to change the way you think in order to change the way you feel. You have to change the way you think in order to change the way you feel.* And I thought, That's it. It's all so simple. And so powerful.

No matter what your circumstances, how high your barriers, or how daunting your challenges, you can change the way you think. And once that happens, you can do anything.

My wish for everyone out there—whether you're just starting out, are at mid-course, or are near the end of your journey—is that you feel happy in what you're doing and blessed by life.

So here's my final word of advice. It's really an affirmation: Live *your* life. Let it happen. Enjoy the ride. And whatever you do, do it from the heart.

Remember, rules *are* made to be broken, *except* when it comes to your health!

Acknowledgments

This is the easiest yet hardest part of the book for me. It's easy to thank those who helped me express myself on these pages but difficult to name them all. If I did, I would need a second volume.

Let me begin with Catherine Whitney, who gently pushed me to reveal what is most important to me. Your literary expertise gave me confidence that I had a story worth sharing with others. This book would have stayed in my mind and heart without your wonderful guidance. Thank you for helping me put it down on paper. I appreciate you never letting me lose sight of the big picture.

Acknowledgments

To all my friends at Hyperion—and you have become my dear friends. First, to Robert Miller. Bob, you live your life with heart, and that is what drew me to Hyperion. I have been asked over the years to write a book like this and always politely declined. But when I sat down with you for the first time, all that changed. We share the same excitement for life and the belief that we all have gifts that can make a true difference.

To my editor, Gretchen Young: I adore you. I got such a big kick out of our conversations. It seems the last thing we would talk about was my book. We would chat about our families, friends—about life. I always walk away from you feeling energized and full of ideas and possibilities. Thank you and everyone at Hyperion for that.

I never understood why people would thank their agents when they received a big award. Now I do. I owe so much to my friends at N.S. Bienstock, especially Peter Goldberg and Richard Leibner. Peter, I'll never forget that you traveled all the way to Mississippi for my father's funeral. You've always been there for me.

Richard, you are a genius. I couldn't believe you

contacted me the morning I filled in as the host of *Good Morning America Sunday* way back when. You were the first to tell me I could make the transition from sports to network news. You said when I was ready, to give you a call. Turned out to be one of the best calls I ever made. You and Peter have helped me navigate the sometimes treacherous waters of broadcasting. I can't wait for our next lunch.

To my colleagues at WDAM in Hattiesburg, Mississippi; WLOX in Biloxi, Mississippi; WSMV in Nashville, Tennessee; and WAGA in Atlanta, Georgia—thank you! It was a privilege to work alongside each and every one of you. Thank you for teaching me and being patient with me. I learned so much from you—lessons I draw upon every day of my professional life.

There is definitely not enough room to heap praise on my ESPN family. I had always dreamed of working at ESPN one day. Reality surpassed my dreams. From the president, George Bodenheimer, to the former president Steve Bornstein; from executives John Walsh, Howard Katz, and Steve Anderson to producers, directors, technicians, researchers, and production assistants—you are simply the best.

Acknowledgments

My fellow *SportsCenter* anchors and reporters— you rock! It was one heck of a ride.

It's such an honor to be a member of the ABC News family. I am in awe of your professionalism, commitment, and humanity. *Good Morning America* is a 24-hour, 365-day-a-year job. The *GMA* staff is relentless, creative, and the hardest-working folks in this sometimes crazy business. Your compassion and humor lift me to incredible heights. What people see every morning on our program is a direct reflection of your tireless dedication. From the bottom of my heart I thank each and every one of you. I love you.

To viewers who have watched me over the years. You have encouraged me more than you could possibly know. Back in the early '80s when I started this amazing journey, you were patient with me. You challenged me to be the best I could be. Many of you have told me that you've laughed with me and you've cried with me. I can only pray that I have inspired you half as much as you've inspired me. I don't take lightly the fact that you have graciously invited me into your homes via television all these years. I hope I've been a good houseguest.

To the people of my home state of Mississippi.

Acknowledgments

Thank you for welcoming the Roberts Family to the Mississippi Coast in 1969. I want you to know how proud I am of you. That pride was magnified after Hurricane Katrina. Your strength and courage in the face of such adversity is beyond admirable. I saw how we came back stronger than ever after Hurricane Camille. Together we'll do it again, and I carry you in my heart always.

To my "Dream Team"—my talented doctors. Albert Knapp, Lauren Cassell, Ruth Oratz, and Roberto Lipsztein. You are simply the best. But it goes beyond your incredible skills as physicians. Your genuine concern, compassion, and devotion to all your patients is exemplary. I'll be forever grateful to you, your wonderful nurses, and loving support staffs. You are all angels!

To my second family, my inner circle, my dear friends. You know my faults and weaknesses and still love me unconditionally. You've shared my highs and helped me get through the lows of life. I know it's not easy being my friend. All the times I have to cancel plans and trips at the last minute because of breaking news. All the early-bird specials I force you to eat because I've got to get to bed early. It's wild when you think that of the billions of people on earth we found one another. Nothing happens by chance. I have no idea where life is going to take us next—but I am comforted knowing we will be by one another's side every step of the way. My dear friends, you make me a better person—and I love you back.

To my siblings—what a blessing you are. I would feel that way about you even if we were not related. I'd like to think I'm the perfect blend of all three of you. My dear brother, Lawrence Edward Roberts II. I know it wasn't easy being the only boy in the family and carrying on as Dad's namesake. Those are mighty big shoes to fill. You blazed your own path with integrity and grace. Butch, you're a good man. Sweet Sally-Ann. You're so sweet, I joke that I get a cavity every time I talk to you. I think what I admire most about you is your genuineness. You're the re al deal. Your uplifting spirit is something to behold. Dorothy, you are by far the most talented one of the bunch— and the one most like Mom. I know with two sisters in TV you sometimes feel overlooked. But I love your feistiness in making your presence felt, not to mention your humor. I greatly admire how all three of you have raised remarkable children—Bianca, Renée,

Lawrence, Judith, Kelly, Jeremiah, Jessica, and Lauren. The circle contines.

Hopefully you saw my dedication to my parents. It's hard to put into words the impact they have had on my life. I tried my best to do that with this book. Daddy, I miss you. Mom, thank you for the shining example you set each and every day. I want to be just like you when I grow up.

Robin Roberts is a co-anchor of *Good Morning America* and one of the most recognized and respected individuals in the media. A native of Pass Christian, Mississippi, she was a college basketball standout and, for more than fifteen years, an anchor of ESPN's award-winning *SportsCenter*. Robin lives in New York City.